I0611698

Orlando Innamorato
of
Matteo Maria Boiardo

Translated into prose
From the Italian of
Francesco Berni
and
interspersed with extracts
in the same stanza as the original by

William Stewart Rose

Table of Contents

To
HENRY RICHARD, LORD HOLLAND,

Who, at a late period of my labours upon the "Furioso,"
suggested the present work as its necessary prologue.

KIND peer, who, mid the tempest of debate,
    Hast gladly wooed and won the Southern muse,
Where, crowned with fruit and flower of mingling hues,
    She in a grove of myrtle keeps her state,
This I had entered by a postern gate,
    Like stranger, who no certain path pursues,
Or garden's lord, that hath his own to choose,
    Hadst thou not shewn a better entrance late :
That portal led me to Morgana's[1] towers,
    Where fierce Orlando found the dame at play;
And though, too fast for me, from fields of flowers,
    She flies to savage waste, and will not stay,
It will content me but to paint her bowers,
    If this be granted by the scornful fay.
William Stewart Rose.

---

[1] See the adventure of Morgana, the type of Fortune, who, flying from her
garden into a wilderness, is taken by Orlando, Book II.

Introduction.

IT is many years since I first entertained a vague idea of translating the Orlando Furioso, and circumstances of little importance to the reader, led me more recently to undertake it in earnest. This work was again laid down; and afterwards resumed at the instance of a distinguished friend; and by an odd coincidence, I am indebted also to the suggestion of another eminent person for the idea of the present translation of the Orlando Innamorato, which, I should observe, is intended to be auxiliary to that, my first and greater undertaking, though I need scarcely say, that the story of Boiardo is a necessary prologue to the poem of Ariosto.

It was my intention to have translated the first mentioned work, exactly upon the model adopted by Tressan in his version of the French romances, a scheme afterwards executed with so much better success, by my late excellent friend, Mr. George Ellis, in his English work of the same description. A further consideration of the subject, however, induced me to imitate them only in their general plan of illustrating a compendious prose translation by extracts, without seeking to add poignancy to this, by what might give a false idea of the tone of my original. I recollected that I stood in a very different predicament from that of either of these authors; that, to compare my work with the one, which is most likely to be familiar to my readers, the 'Specimens of early English Romances,' the originals are composed in a spirit of gravity which can hardly be confused with the gay style of the translator, and therefore nobody can be misled by the vein of pleasantry which runs through Mr. Ellis's work, and which is sure to be exclusively ascribed to the author of the Rifacimento. This, however, would possibly not be the case with me, as the Innamorato is in a great measure a humourous work, of which I might give a false impression, by infusing into it a different species of wit, from that which distinguishes it; a consideration which induced me to adopt the scheme I have pursued in the following sheets. This project is to give a mere ground-plan of the

Gothic edifice of Boiardo, upon a small scale, accompanied with some elevations and sections of the chambers; which I have sought to colour after jny original : or, (to speak more plainly,) the reader is to look for the mere story in my prose abridgement, while he may form some notion of its tone and style, from the stanzas with which it is interspersed.

The story indeed, which seems most likely to interest the English reader, is that which took a strong possession of the imagination of Milton, who refers with more apparent enthusiasm to the Innamorato, than to the Furioso, and whose apparent preference is justifiable, if a richer stream of invention, and more consummate art in its distribution, are legitimate titles to admiration.

In this latter qualification more especially, Boiardo, however inferior as a poet, must be considered as a superior artist to Ariosto; and weaving as complicated a web as his successor, it is curious to observe how much he excels him as a story-teller. The tales, indeed, of Ariosto, (and the want of connexion among these is, in my eyes, his most essential defect) are so many loose episodes, which may be compared to parallel streams, flowing towards one reservoir, but through separate and independent channels. Those of Boiardo, on the contrary, are like waters, that, however they may diverge, preserve their relation to the parent river, to which their accession always seems necessary, and with which they reunite, previous to its discharging its contents into their common resting-place. A short example may serve to illustrate what I have laid down. A damsel in the Innamorato relates to Rinaldo the adventures of two worthies named Iroldo and Prasildo, a narration which is interrupted, and which, though good in itself, at first appears to be an insulated episode. Rinaldo, however, afterwards falls in with Iroldo and his friend; and this history, thus resumed, unites itself naturally with that of the paladin. It is thus that all the stories are dove-tailed one into the other, and form a mosaic, as striking from the nice union of its parts, as from the brilliancy of its colours.

Boiardo's art, though here indeed he cannot be said to excel Ariosto, is as conspicuous also in the direction of the strange under-current of allegory which pervades his poem, as it is in the distribution of his stream of story; while the sort of esoteric doctrines conveyed by it, gives a mysterious interest even to what we imperfectly comprehend.

Such indeed is the case with many of the fables of the Odyssey, and even of the Iliad; where the allegory, moreover, is always subservient to poetry, and poetry is never made subservient to allegory. This remarkable piece of judgment in the Greek poet has, I think, been well imitated both by Boiardo and Ariosto, and it is the neglect of this principle which has made allegory so often offensive in the Faery Queene of Spenser. The obtrusive nature of this has been well compared by Mr. George Ellis, in his Specimens of the early English poets, to a ghost in day-light. It is, moreover, destructive to all character; for Spenser's heroes being mere abstract personifications of some virtue or vice, we almost always know what they are to do, though their actions are often unnatural, if considered as the actions of human beings. Hence it is that we are never entertained with pictures of manners in the Faery Queen, while these form one of the great charms of the poems with which I am contrasting it.

It may however be said with justice, that we are to ascribe this more picturesque effect of allegory, rather to the spirit of the age than to that of the fabulist. For it is perhaps true that all early fable is purely allegorical; that this is by degrees mixed up with other circumstances, and it is in this mixed character that it is most conducive to poetical effect. But in a later age and later process of refinement, when there is a greater tendency to abstract, allegory is stript of her adventitious ornaments, and is at last forced upon us in poetry, painting, and sculpture, unveiled, or unencompassed by that sort of pleasing halo which is necessary to give her effect.

But whether we are to ascribe Boiardo's success in this particular to the character of his age, or to his own superior judgment, there is, I think, no doubt about the fact, and there is, I think, as little difficulty in conceding to my author, upon other grounds, the praise of skill in executing the singular work of which he was the architect.

This extraordinary man was Matteo Maria Boiardo, count of Scandiano, and a native of Reggio in the Modenese, who flourished in the beginning of the sixteenth century. These are circumstances the more worthy of mention, as some of them tend to explain what may seem most strange in the composition of the Innamorato; such as the provincial character of the diction, and more especially that careless and almost contemptuous tone between jest and earnest, which distinguishes his poem. It is doubtless on this account that Ugo Foscolo observes, in an ingenious critique on the Italian romantic poets, in the Quarterly Review,[2] that he tells his story in the tone of a feudal baron; thus applying to him more justly what M. de Balzac has objected to another; of whom he says, "qu'il s'est comporte dans son poe'me comme un prince dans ses etats. C'est en vertu de cette souverainte qu'il ne reconnoit point les lois, et qu'il se met au dessus du droit commun."

After speaking of the mode in which he arranged his work, it is a natural transition to the substance with which Boiardo built. This shews strong internal evidence[3] of having been taken, in the main, from the old French romances of Charlemagne, or rather

---

[2] In an article purporting to be a review of Whistlecraft's poem, (now entitled The Monks and Giants,) and The Court and Parliament of Beasts.

[3] A single circumstance, which I cite, because it can be appreciated by every body, would convince me that such stories as are to be found in the Innamorato, were not the growth of Boiardo's century. No author of that age could have imagined the friendly ties of alliance and consanguinity between Christians and paynims, though such fictions are justified by facts: thus we learn from Gibbon that like relations existed between Greeks and Turks, and (as we are informed by Mr. Lockhart, in the preface to his Spanish Ballads, a work which presents as striking pictures of manners as of passion) between Spaniards and Moors. Nor need such things surprise us, though the barriers which now separate Christian and Mahomedan, render them impossible. Nations are like individuals, and when they are brought into close and constant intercourse, of whatever kind, their passions, good or bad, must be kindled by the contact.

from Italian works, raised upon their foundation. Hoole mentions one of these, called Aspramonte, &c., of uncertain date, and we have the titles of two others, which were anterior to the Innamorato, one called Li fat ft di Carlo Magno c del Paladini di Francia, printed in 1481; the other printed in 1491, and entitled La Historia real di Francici) die tratta deifatti dei Paladini e di Carlo Magno in sei libri. Some indeed would seem to deny that Boiardo had dug in these mines, and would wish us to believe, that he not only compounded but manufactured the materials with which he wrought. Such at least would appear to have been the drift of one, who observes that Agramant, Sacripant and Gradassso were names of certain of the vassals of Scandiano. But if he means to insinuate by this, that Boiardo was not also indebted to the other source for his fictions and characters, as well might a critic of to-day, contend that the author of the Monks and Giants., who writes under the name of Whistlecraft, had not borrowed the idea of their cause of quarrel from Pulci, because he has given ridiculous modern names to some of his giants; or that he had not taken the leaders amongst his dramatis persona from the romances of the Round Table, because he has conferred " two leopards' faces," that is, his own arms, on the single knight, who perishes in Sir Tristram's successful expedition.

But if Boiardo has apparently taken his principal fictions from the romances of Charlemagne, he has also resorted to other known quarries, and ransacked classical as well as romantic fable for materials.

This edifice, so constructed, which Boiardo did not live to finish, soon underwent alteration and repairs. The first were made by Niccolo degli Agostini, and later in the same century a second and more celebrated rifacimento of it, from which this translation is composed, was produced by Francesco Berni; whose name has given a distinctive epithet to the style of poetry, in which he excelled, and of which he is vulgarly supposed to have been the inventor.

This man was born of poor but noble parents, in a small town of Tuscany. He entered the church, to which he had evidently no disposition, as a means of livelihood, and, though as unqualified for servitude as for the discharge of his clerical duties, spent the better part of his life in dependence. He appears, however, to have been blessed with a vein of cheerfulness, which, seconded by a lively imagination, enabled him to beguile the wearisome nature of occupations, which were uncongenial to him; and of this he has left many monuments in sonnets and pieces in terza rima, (styled in Italian capitoli,) consisting of satires and various species of ludicrous composition. The titles of many of these sufficiently attest their whimsicality, such as his Capitoli sugli Orinali, sidle Anguille, his Eulogy of the Plague, &c. &c. But the mode in which he has handled this last subject, will give the best insight into the character of his humour. Having premised that different persons gave a preference to different seasons — as the poet to the spring, and the reveller to the autumn, he observes, that one may well like the season of flowers, or the other that of fruits; but that, for his part, he preferred the time of plague. He then backs his predilection by a rehearsal of the advantages attending this visitation; observing that a man is in such times free from solicitations of borrowers or creditors, and safe from disagreeable companions; that he has elbow-room at church and market, and can then only be said to be in the full possession of his natural liberty. He has rung all sorts of changes on this theme, and nothing can be more humorous than his details.

These are worked up with singular powers of diction, set off by great apparent facility of style, and are no less remarkable for music of rythm, richness of rhyme, and a happy boldness of expression. In this respect there is some analogy, though no likeness, between Berni and Dryden; and the real merits of both are therefore imperfectly estimated by foreigners, and even by the generality of their own countrymen. Many Italians, indeed, consider Berni as a mere buffoon, which the English reader will think less extraordinary, when he hears (as Lord Glenbervie[4] observes, I think, in his notes to Ricciardetto,) that such an opinion has been entertained in Italy, even with regard to Ariosto.

Better reasons may seem to palliate such a mistake of the real poetical character of Berni, than of that of Ariosto. Some of these are of a general description, and others of a nature more peculiarly applicable to his case. We may observe, as to the first, that whoever indulges his wit, in whatever species of composition, is usually misjudged; for wit, in the sight of the world, overlays all the other qualities of an author, in whatever act or pursuit he may be engaged. Thus a great English painter, single in his walk, and distinguished by his various powers, is looked upon by the multitude as a mere caricaturist, even where caricature is intended by him only as a foil to beauty; and orators have for the same reason sunk into jesters in the opinion of the mob, though they may have been equally distinguished for argumentative discussion or pathetic effect.

But other and more particular circumstances have tended to fix this character upon Berni. Few men have a delicate perception of familiar expression, and still fewer yet have a nice feeling of the delicacies of prosody,

Untwisting all the links that tie
The secret chain of harmony.

Now it is for the bold, however dexterous, use of language, and rythm, that Berni is principally distinguished; and hence, as the means through which he works are imperfectly understood by the majority of his readers, his object has been frequently mistaken. I should cite, in illustration of this, his description of a storm at sea, which has been often deemed burlesque, but in which the poet would be more justly considered as working a fine effect by unwonted means.

---

[4] I state this on Lord Glenbervie's sole authority, which is, however, a weighty one. Such an opinion was probably current when he first knew Italy; but I should imagine it could hardly be entertained at present.

Let us try this question by the rules of analogy. Men in all countries resemble one another in the main, and where they are not guided by a natural taste and judgment, lean upon some rule, which is to direct them as an infallible guide. Depending upon this, they seldom consider that it may be narrow, or of insufficient support. Thus an Englishman who has learned to think about verse, by the help of a few simple precepts[5], which he believes to be absolute, is taught to look upon the double rhyme as suited only to burlesque poetry. Yet Drummond's

"Methought desponding nightingales did borrow,
Plaint of my plaint, and sorrow of my sorrow;"
and the description of him, who
"Saw with wonder,
Vast magazines of ice and piles of thunder,"[6]

might be cited to prove what widely different effects are produced by the same weapon, as it s differently wielded. But, impressed with the notions of the laws of verse which I have specified, that is, not knowing that almost all such metrical rules as have been alluded to, are merely conditional, some Italians[7], and certainly, almost all English readers of Italian poetry, suppose the triple rhyme, (la rima sdrucciola] or dactyl, as it is called by us, to be as exclusively applied to ludicrous composition in Italian, as the double rhyme is imagined to be in English; and this is perhaps one cause why some of Berni's stanzas, which abound in triple rhymes, have been so utterly misconceived in England.

---

[5] For example, there is no rule deemed more absolute, and yet there is none which admits more exceptions than the maxim forbidding a line of ten monosyllables. For monosyllables, in French and English, are often such only to the eye, such words being frequently, in both languages, melted into each other. Hence many good English verses consist of ten words, as that of Dryden, which will be in the recollection of every body,
"Arms and the man I sing, &c."
and the French cite as beautiful a line of Racine, which is composed of twelve,
"Lej ur n'est pas plus pur rjue k fond de moil civiir."
[6] I quote from memory.
[7] Thus Goldoni in one of his comedies introduces a man improvising in triple rhymes for the sake of producing a ludicrous effect. Goldoui, however, it must be confessed, is no authority in questions of language or of versification.

Yet Berni and Ariosto have frequently employed the versi sdruccioli where they have aimed at a bold or pathetic effect, though they have also undoubtedly been used by them to heighten that of comic or satirical composition. Caro the cotemporary of Berni is even profuse of triple rhymes in his translation of the AEneid; lyric poets, after the example of Chiabrera, often insert them in the sublimest of their odes; and one, who lately died full of years, managed the rime sdrucciole so easily, as to compose whole poems with them, and with such dignity, both of versification and expression, as (in the opinion of a distinguished Italian friend already cited) to vie with Tasso and Petrarch.

Now let a man keep such doctrines in mind; let him come to the consideration of Berni's storm with a memory imbued with the sights and sounds seen and heard in one; let him consider all circumstances of metre, not absolutely, but conditionally; that is, in their relation to each other and the thing described, and he will then, I believe, enter into the real spirit in which the poet executed this description, and contemplate him with very different eyes from those with which he viewed him before.

Another cause of misconception, to which I have already alluded, has probably more misled the mob of readers of Italian poetry, natives as well as foreigners. I mean the language of Berni; and as to this, certainly few very few, are capable of appreciating his skill, or even of making out his track. There is indeed, I believe, no poet of any country, who has attempted so difficult a flight; a flight of unwearied wing, struck out with courage, and maintained only by the most incessant exertion and care.

Traces of these are seen in what may be called the charts on which he has pricked out his course, and which, I understand, witness as much to his diligence, as Ariosto's attest the care with which he accomplished his most extraordinary voyage. The documents to which I allude, are the original MSS. of the Innamorato, preserved at Brescia. As I was ignorant of the existence of these, during two residences which I made in Italy, I can only speak of them on the testimony of others; but an Italian critic, whom I have often quoted, and from whose authority upon such points I would almost say there was no appeal, once assured me these are as much blotted as those of Ariosto at Ferrara; and that Berni seems to have usually clothed his thoughts in ornate language at first, which he rejected on after-consideration, simplifying, but at the same time improving, his diction, as he proceeded, till he arrived at that exquisite happiness of expression, that curiosa felicitas, which makes his principal charm. It is hence that he is the most untranslatable of authors; since in copying him, it is not only a question of imitating colours, but the fine and more elaborate touches of a peculiar pencil.

While, however, it is clear that the versification and diction make the great charms of the Innamorato) these beauties should not throw his other excellencies into shade; and the openings of the different cantos, which he has engrafted on the original work of Boiardo, sometimes original, and sometimes imitated from the older poets, are not greatly inferior to those which Ariosto has prefixed to the several cantos of the Furioso, in imitation of him; no, not even in the higher claims of poetical merit.

These sometimes consist of moral reflections, arising out of the narrative; and the following may remind the reader of one of those little gems scattered through the plays of Shakspeare :

Who steals a bugle-horn, a ring, a steed,
Or such like worthless thing, has some discretion.
'Tis petty larceny. Not such his deed
Who robs us of our fame, our best possession;
And he who takes our labour's worthiest meed,
May well be deemed a felon by profession;
Who so much more our hate and scourge de — serves,
As from the rule of right he wider swerves.

Sometimes indulging in a declamation against vices or follies, he makes his satire more poignant by allusions to some prevalent practice of the day: thus, in a sally against avarice, he attacks those who masqued it under the disguise of hypocrisy in the following stanza :

This other, under show of an adviser

And practiser of what is strict and right;
But being in effect a rogue and miser,
Cloisters a dozen daughters out of sight :
And fain would have the pretty creatures wiser
Than their frail sisters; but mistakes them quite;
For they are like the rest, and set the group
Of monks, and priests, and abbots, cock-a-hoop.

The following extract, illustrating a philosophical dogma of his age, taken from the opening of the forty-sixth canto, is of another description, and may serve as a specimen of the variety of his vein, and the odd ingenuity with which he winds in and out of his argument; sometimes bearing up for his harbour when in the middle of a digression; and then, when he seems to feel himself sure of a retreat, indulging in a new sally, in which he however never entirely loses sight of his port.

I.

He who the name of little world applied
To man, in this approved his subtle wit:
Since, save it is not round, all things beside
Exactly with this happy symbol fit;
And I may say that long and deep, and wide
And middling, good and bad, are found in it.
Here too, the various elements combined
Are dominant; snow, rain, and mist and wind.

2.

Now clear, now overcast. 'Tis there its land
Will yield no fruit; here bears a rich supply :
As the mixt soil is marie, or barren sand;
And haply here too moist, or there too dry.
Here foaming hoarse, and there with murmur bland,
Streams glide, or torrents tumble from on high.
Such of man's appetites convey the notion :
Since these are infinite, and still in motion.

3.

Two solid dikes the invading streams repel,
The one is Reason, and the other Shame.

The torrents, if above their banks they swell,
Wit and discretion are too weak to tame.
The crystal waters, which so smoothly well,
Are appetites of things, devoid of blame.
Those winds, and rains, and snows, and night, and day,
Ye learned clerks, divine them as ye may.

4.

Among these elements, misfortune wills
Our nature should have most of earth : for she,
Moved by what influence heaven or sun instils,
Is subject to their power; nor less are we.
In her, this star or that, in barren hills
Produces mines in rich variety :
And those who human nature wisely scan
May this discern peculiarly in man.

5.

Who would believe that various minerals grew,
And many metals, in our rugged mind;
From gold to nitre ? Yet the thing is true;
But, out, alas ! the rub is how to find
This ore. Some letters and some wealth pursue,
Some fancy steeds, some dream, at ease reclined;
These song delights, and those the cittern's sound,
Such are the mines which in our world abound.

6.

As these are worthier, more or less, so they
Abound with lead or gold; and practised wight,
The various soil accustomed to survey,
Is fitted best to find the substance bright.
And such in our Apulia is the way
They heal those suffering from the spider's bite;
Who strange vagaries play, like men possessed;
Tarantulated[8], as 'tis there express'd.

---

[8] The Tarantula is now known to be harmless. The cause of its supposed mischievous effects, and the efficacy of the mode of curing them are perhaps easily explained. People are in all countries (though they are imagined to be

7.

For this, 'tis needful, touching sharp or flat,
To seek a sound which may the patients please;
Who, when they find the merry music pat,
Dance till they sweat away the foul disease.
And thus who should allure this man or that,
And still with various offer tempt and tease,
I wot, in little time, would ascertain
And sound each different mortal's mine and vein.

8.

'Twos so Brunello with Rogero wrought,
Who offered him the armour and the steed.
Thus by the cunning Greek his aid was bought,
Who laid fair Ilion smoking on the mead.
Which was of yore in clearer numbers taught;
Nor shall I now repeat upon my reed,
Who from the furrow let my plough-share stray,
Unheeding how the moments glide away.

9.

As the first pilot by the shore did creep,
Who launched his boat upon the billows dark,
And where the liquid ocean was least deep,
And without sails impelled his humble barque;
But seaward next, where foaming waters leap,

---

peculiarly so in England) exposed to attacks of melancholy, which arise out of some physical cause, whether indigestion, or other bodily complaint. The doctors of Calabria attributed this to the sting of the tarantula, which is assuredly not more extravagant than a popular English medical author's ascribing jaundice to the bite of a mad dog. The patient, delighted to find a cause for his complaint, was easily, by leading questions, brought to recollect that he had, at some time or other, felt a prick, which probably proceeded from the sting of a tarantula. Dancing was the remedy prescribed; and this, as exciting the animal spirits, fee. may very well have operated a cure of the real disease. The patients were to be played to, as Berni states, till a tune was struck which pleased their fancy, and animated them to exertion. The Tarantella, an air supposed to be particularly stimulating in such a case, is still a popular dance in the south of Italy. Modern philosophers have found out that the tarantula has no venom.

By little and by little steered his ark,
With nothing but the wind and stars to guide,
And round about him glorious wonders spied.

10.

Thus I, who still have sung a humble strain,
And kept my little barque within its bounds,
Now find it fit to launch into the main,
And sing the fearful warfare, which resounds
Where Africa pours out her swarthy train,
And the wide world with mustered troops abounds;
And, fanning fire and forge, each land and nation
Sends forth the dreadful note of preparation.

THE next extract I shall give, though it commences with his favourite figure of the barque, will serve as a specimen of a different style. It forms the opening of the second book. The two first lines the reader will trace to Dante, and will find in the remainder a translation of the AEneadum Genetrix of Lucretius.

1.

Launched on a deeper sea, my pinnace, rear
Thy sail, prepared to plough the billows dark;
And you, ye lucid stars, by whom I steer
My feeble vessel to its destined mark,
Shine forth upon her course benign and clear,
And beam propitious on the daring barque
About to stem an ocean so profound :
While I your praises and your works resound.

2.

O, holy mother of AEneas ! O,
Daughter of Jove ! thou bliss of gods above
And men beneath; VENUS, who makest grow
Green herb and plant, and fillest all with love;
Thou creatures that would else be cold and slow,
Dost with thy sovereign instinct warm and move,
Thou dost all jarring things in peace unite
The world's eternal spirit, life and light.

3.

At thine appearance storm and rain have ceased,
And zephyr has unlocked the genial ground;
Leap the wild herds; 'tis wanton nature's feast,
And the green woods with singing birds resound;
While by strange pleasure stung, the savage beast
Lives but for love; what time their greenwood round
All creatures rove, or couch upon the sward,
Discord and hate forgot, in sweet accord.

4.

Thee, kind and gentle star ! thy suppliant prays;
To thee I sue by every bolt which flies
Thro' the fifth planet[9], melting with thy rays,
When panting on thy lap the godhead lies,
And lock'd within thine arms, with upward gaze,
Feeds on thy visage his desiring eyes :
That thou wilt gain for me his grace, and grown
Propitious, with his grace accord thine own.

5.

Since 'tis of thee I sing, as I have said,
And only of thy praise and pleasures dream;
Well pleased I to this fruitful field was led,
And sure I could not choose a sweeter theme.
Thou too, that down thy clear and ample bed
Dost run with grateful murmur, RAPID STREAM,
Awhile from thine impetuous course refrain,
While on thy banks I tune my mingled strain.

In the concluding address to the river, he apostrophizes the
Adige, on whose banks he might be said to be writing, as he was
then living hi the town of Verona, which is watered by it, in the
service of the Cardinal di Bibbiena.

One more specimen of his poetical prefaces, and I have done.
It is the introduction to his third book; and in this too the reader,
who will recognize a passage of the ars poetica of Horace, may

---

[9] Mars.

observe how well Berni translates and applies his classical recollections.

I.

As they, who their unhappy task fulfil
In mines of England, Hungary, and Spain,
The deeper that they dig the mountain, still
Find richer treasure and securer gain;
And as wayfaring man who climbs a hill,
Surveys, as he ascends, a wider plain,
And shores and oceans open on his eye,
Exalted nearer to the starry sky :

2.

So in this book, indited for your pleasure,
If you believe and listen to my lore,
You, in advancing, shall discern new treasure,
And catch new lights and landscapes evermore.
Then by no former scale my promise measure,
Nor judge this strain by that which went before:
Since still my caves and rugged rocks unfold
A richer vein of jewels, pearls, and gold.

3.

And he who winds about my mountain's side,
Still spies new lands and seas, a glorious sight,
If patient industry and courage guide
Him from the valley to the frowning height.
Like prospect was the poet's who supplied
Flame out of smoke, instead of smoke from light;
With wise Ulysses' acts to fill our ears,
To the more wonderment of him who hears.

So much for the poetry of Berni. His life was not such as reflected any lustre on his works. This, if we reject some foul imputations cast upon him, was, to say the least of it, disreputable. It is, however, certain, that being at last established in a canonry at Florence, he lived there in high and accomplished society. This fact, however, in a profligate age, like that in which he flourished, proves nothing in his favour; and, if we listened to the stories of his biographers, we might suppose him even to have been courted for some of his vicious propensities : for one of these writers tells us he was excited by the cardinal Ippolito de' Medici to poison the duke Alexander, against whom he had a private pique; another, would have us believe that he was tempted by the duke to poison the cardinal; and (to complicate the matter yet more) that the cardinal or the duke, or both, had poison administered to Berni himself, upon his refusal. The dates, however, of their respective deaths, are at variance with these strange assertions; and if such certain means of contradiction were wanting, the internal evidence of Berni's character, however vicious, might be almost sufficient to refute such improbable calumnies. It may be said, indeed, that perhaps no one was ever selected as a probable agent of guilt, who seems to have been so little capable of engaging in the sort of crimes which were expected of him.

As a proof of this we might almost refer to the picture which he has given of himself, and which carries with it every warrant of resemblance. In one of the cantos of the last book of the Innamorato, he describes a number of persons as having become the victims of a tairy, of whom they afterwards remain the voluntary prisoners. Among these he has, in imitation of certain painters, introduced himself with another known character of the day : a circumstance which, together with the nature of the episode, might lead one to suspect that Thomson was indebted to this fiction for his Castle of Indolence. He has, however, given the tenants of his " bowers of ease," a character so much more intellectual than that of Berni's actors, that he may very fairly pretend to the praise of original composition, even if his work be an imitation instead of a mere accidental coincidence; which I am more tempted to believe.[10] But I draw the curtain of Berni's picture.

---

[10] I do not recollect any authority for Thomson's having been conversant with Italian poetry; and I think that a view of his works would lead to a contrary supposition. Thus I should say that though no man could copy what he actually saw with a nicer hand or eye, no man had more need of study in the

Book III. Canto VII.

36.

A boon companion to increase this crew
By chance, a gentle Florentine, was led;
A Florentine, altho' the father who
Begot him, in the Casentine was bred;
Who nigh become a burgher of his new
Domicile, there was well content to wed;
And so in Bibbiena wived, which ranks
Among the pleasant towns on Arno's banks. "

37.

At Lamporecchio, he of whom I write
Was born, for dumb Masetto[II] fam'd of yore,
Thence roam'd to Florence; and in piteous plight
There sojourned till nineteen, like pilgrim poor;
And shifted thence to Rome, with second flight
Hoping some succour from a kinsman's store;
A cardinal allied to him by blood,
And one that neither did him harm nor good.

38.

He to the nephew passed, this patron dead,
Who the same measure as his uncle meted;
And then again in search of better bread,
With empty bowels from his house retreated;
And hearing, for his name and fame were spread,

Italian school of ideal picture than this English poet. Jn his drawings from nature his colouring is as inimitable as his design; and his bird, who
"Shivers every feather with desire,"
is painted with the precision as well as the force of the Flemish pencil. Yet he has personified Autumn as
"Crowned with the sickle and the wheaten sheaf,"
thus putting on his head what should have been in his hand, and presenting us a ludicrous figure surmounted by a " crumpled horn." No Italian poet would have painted from nature with Thomson's marvellous precision; and no Italian poet would have committed such gross offences against propriety as he has, in his imaginary pictures.

[II] See Boccaccio.

The praise of one who serv'd the pope repeated,
And in the Roman court Datario hight,
He hired himself to him to read and write.
39.
This trade the unhappy man believed he knew;
But this belief was, like the rest, a bubble,
Since he could never please the patron, who
Fed him, nor ever once was out of trouble.
The worse he did, the more he had to do,
And only made his pain and penance double :
And thus, with sleeves and bosom stuffed with papers,
Wasted his wits, and lived oppressed with vapours.
40.
Add for his mischief (whether 'twas his little
Merit, misfortune, or his want of skill)
Some cures he farmed produced him not a tittle,
And only were a source of plague and ill.
Fire, water, storm, or devil, sacked vines and victual,
Whether the luckless wretch would tythe or till.
Some pensions too, which he possessed, were nought,
And, like the rest, produced him not a groat.
4I.
This notwithstanding, he his miseries slighted,
Like happy man, who not too deeply feels;
And all, but most the Roman lords, delighted,
Content in spite of tempests, writs, or seals,
And oftentimes, to make them mirth, recited
Strange chapters upon urinals and eels;[12]
And other mad vagaries would rehearse,
That he had hitched, Heaven help him ! into verse.
42.
His mood was choleric, and his tongue was vicious,
But he was praised for singleness of heart;
Not taxed as avaricious or ambitious,
Affectionate, and frank, and void of art;

---

[12] See his Cajntoli sugli Orinali, Sulk dtiqitille, etc.

A lover of his friends, and unsuspicious;
But where he hated, knew no middle part;
And men his malice by his love might rate :
But then he was more prone to love than hate.
43.
To paint his person, this was thin and dry;
Well sorting it, his legs were spare and lean;
Broad was his visage, and his nose was high,
While narrow was the space that was between
His eye-brows sharp; and blue his hollow eye,
Which for his bushy beard had not been seen,
But that the master kept this thicket clear'd,
At mortal war with moustache and with board.
44.
No one did ever servitude detest
Like him; though servitude was still his dole :
Since fortune or the devil did their best
To keep him evermore beneath controul.
While, whatsoever was his patron's hest,
To execute it went against his soul;
His service would he freely yield, unasked,
But lost all heart and hope, if he were tasked.
45.
Nor musick, hunting-match, nor mirthful measure,
Nor play, nor other pastime moved him aught;
And if 'twas true that horses gave him pleasure,
The simple sight of them was all he sought,
Too poor to purchase; and his only treasure
His naked bed : his pastime to do nought
But tumble there, and stretch his weary length,
And so recruit his spirits and his strength,
46.
Worn with the trade he long was used to slave in,
So heartless and so broken down was he;
He deemed he could not find a readier haven,
Or safer port from that tempestuous sea;

Nor better cordial to recruit his craven
And jaded spirit, when he once was free,
Than to betake himself to bed, and do
Nothing, and mind and matter so renew.

47.

On this as on an art, he would dilate,
In good set terms, and styled his bed a vest,
Which, as the wearer pleased, was small or great,
And of whatever fashion liked him best;
A simple mantle, or a robe of state;
With that a gown of comfort and of rest :
Since whosoever slipt his daily clothes
For this, put off with these all worldly woes.

48.

He by the noise and lights and music jaded
Of that long revel, and the tramp and tread,
(Since every guest in his desires was aided,
And knaves performed their will as soon as said,)
Found out a chamber which was uninvaded,
And bade those varlets there prepare a bed,
Garnished with bolsters and with pillows fair,
At its four borders, and exactly square.

49.

This was six yards across by mensuration,
With sheets and curtains bleached by wave and breeze,
With a silk quilt for farther consolation,
And all things fitting else : tho' hard to please,
Six souls therein had found accommodation
But this man sighed for elbow-room and ease,
And here as in a sea was fain to swim,
Extending at his pleasure length and limb.

50.

By chance with him, to join the fairy's train,
A Frenchman and a cook was thither brought;
One that had served in court with little gain,
Though he with sovereign care and cunning wrought.

For him, prepared with sheet and counterpane,
Another bed was, like his fellow's, sought :
And 'twixt the two, sufficient space was seen
For a fair table to be placed between.
51.
Upon this table, for the pair to dine,
Were savoury viands piled, prepared with art;
All ordered by this master-cook divine;
Boiled, roast, ragouts and jellies, paste and tart :
But soups and syrups pleased the Florentine,
Who loathed fatigue like death, and for his part,
Brought neither teeth nor fingers into play;
But made two varlets feed him as he lay.
52.
Here couchant, nothing but his head was spied,
Sheeted and quilted to the very chin;
And needful food a serving man supplied
Thro' pipe of silver, placed the mouth within.
Meantime the sluggard moved no part beside,
Holding all motion else were shame and sin;
And (so his spirits and his health were broke)
Not to fatigue this organ, seldom spoke.
53.
The cook was master Peter hight, and he
Had tales at will to while away the day;
To him the Florentine : " Those fools, pardie,
"Have little wit, who dance that endless Hay;"
And Peter in return, " I think with thee."
Then with some merry story backed the say;
Swallowed a mouthful and turned round in bed;
And so, by starts, talked, turned, and slept, and fed.
54.
And so the time these careless comrades cheated,
And still, without a change, ate, drank, and slept
Nor by the calendar their seasons meeted,
Nor register of days or sennights kept :

No dial told the passing hours, which fleeted,
Nor bell was heard; nor servant overstept
The threshold (so the pair proclaimed their will)
To bring them tale or tidings, good or ill.
55.
Above all other curses, pen and ink
Were by the Tuscan held in hate and scorn;
Who, worse than any loathsome sight or stink,
Detested pen and paper, ink and horn :
So deeply did a deadly venom sink,
So festered in his flesh a rankling thorn;
While, night and day, with heart and garments rent,
Seven weary years the wretch in writing spent.
56.
Of all their ways to baffle time and tide,
This seems the strangest of their waking dreams :
Couched on their back, the two the rafters eyed,
And taxed their drowsy wits to count the beams;
"Tis thus they mark at leisure, which is wide,
Which short, or which of due proportion seems;
And which worm-eaten are, and which are sound,
And if the total sum is odd or round.[13]

Having in the preceding part of this introduction, given
some account of the mode in which I have executed my task as a
translator, it may be expected that I should give some information
respecting my labours as an editor. To speak frankly, I have none
to give : having annexed no commentary, or, at least,
nothingworthy of being called a commentary, to this work. Some
readers may, perhaps, think I have in this neglected my duty, and
reproach me with not having pointed out the sources from which
many of the fictions in the Innamorato are borrowed, or at least
the points of resemblance which may be found between many of
these and other ancient stories. It appeared, however, to me, that
my readers were as likely as myself to be conversant with

---

[13] I have already given a loose translation of this part of Berni's acccount of
himself in the Court of Bensts.

incidents to be found in the Spectator, Persian Talcs, Arabian Nighfs, and Bibltotheque Orientate. Others who will, perhaps, thank me for sparing them such a display of common-place knowledge may, however, think I have erred in having done nothing to illustrate the allegory of the Innamorato. If I have not, the omission has arisen from a conviction of the inutility of such an attempt. I have read much that has been written upon the allegory of the Furioso, yet never met with any explanation of it, which I considered as satisfactory to myself, though I was persuaded that the commentators were right. Holding obscurity to be one source of the sublime in this branch of imagination, though I will not venture to extend the position further, it appears to me that the reader always best fills up an indistinct outline, according to his own fancy, and is more likely to derive pleasure from doing so, than from a solution which usually presents him with something very different from what he had preconceived. It is this consideration which has restrained me from doing more than throwing out a few ideas which suggested themselves on some parts of Boiardo's allegory, and no wish to avoid any trouble which I might have thought satisfactorily bestowed on it. Still less have I been influenced by any fear of that ridicule which is so readily discharged upon Italian commentators, or those who report their lucubrations; for I can safely say, that I should have pursued the research to which I have alluded, if I had thought I could have done so with any satisfaction to myself, though I had met with no better recompence than that of being compared to the ass who carried off the dead body of the sphynx, after her enigma had been unriddled, and she herself slain by OEdipus.

Book I.

Argument.

Gradasso, king of Sericane, meditates the invasion of France, in order to obtain Bayardo and Durindana. In the mean time Charlemagne is holding a court plenar at Paris; where the appearance of Angelica excites much confusion amid the assembled knights. She returns towards her own kingdom, pursued by Orlando and Rinaldo. Rinaldo having, however, drunk of the waters of Disdain, while she has unfortunately tasted those of Love, is seized with loathing for the damsel, and is, in his turn, followed in vain by her, whom he before pursued. He is now sent by Charlemagne in defence of Marsilius, king of Spain, whose territories were invaded by Gradasso. in his progress towards France. He is here separated from his army by a device of Malagigi, his own brother, who is become the tool of Angelica, and his troops, left without their leader, return home. Marsilius, in consequence of this desertion, buys peace of Gradasso, by assisting him in his invasion of France. Here Charlemagne and his paladins are made prisoners in a thorough rout of the Christian army. Gradasso, however, offers him peace and liberty for himself and followers, on the delivery of Bayardo, who had been brought back from Spain by the French troops, and on his promise to send him Durindana as soon as it is in his power. Charlemagne of course consents, and sends to Paris for the horse. This is, however, refused by Astolpho, who had taken upon himself the government of the city, and who sends a defiance to Gradasso. They meet, and the Indian king is unhorsed, who, in compliance with the conditions of a previous agreement, frees his prisoners and returns to Sericana. Astolpho, too, dissatisfied with the conduct of Charlemagne, departs from France. He now enrolls himself amongst the defenders of Angelica, besieged by Agrican in Albracca, in which warfare he is made prisoner; Orlando, with other puissant knights, takes the same side, and slays Agrican in single combat. On the other part, Rinaldo (whose hatred to Angelica equals his former love) joins the camp of the besiegers, and a desperate battle is fought between him and Orlando. Angelica, however, still enamoured of Rinaldo, separates them and dispatches Orlando upon a perilous quest. Many other adventures are achieved by these and other knights, and many episodes are connected with the two principal actions of the book, viz. the invasion of France, and the war before Albracca.

THE story says that there reigned formerly in parts beyond India, a mighty monarch, who was moreover so valiant and powerful in war that no one could stand against him; he was named Gradasso; he had the face and heart of a dragon, and was in stature a giant. But, as it often happens to the greatest and to the richest, to long for what they cannot have, and thus to lose what they already possess, this king could not rest content without Durindana the sword of Orlando, and Bayardo the horse of Rinaldo. To obtain which, he determined to war upon France, and for this expedition chose one hundred and fifty thousand horsemen.

But the author suspends the further mention of this monarch, of whom we shall soon again hear, to speak of Charlemagne, who had ordered magnificent jousts, and summoned thither all and singular his barons. And to this court plenar, besides his paladins, and greater and lesser vassals of the crown, were bid all strangers, baptized or infidel, then sojourning at Paris. Amongst the guests were the giant Grandonio, Ferrau, the king Balugantes, a relation of Charlemagne, Isolier and Serpentin, who were companions, and many others.

And now was the day when the great festival was to begin with a sumptuous banquet, made by Charlemagne, who assisted at it in his royal robes, and entertained, between Christians and Pagans, twenty-two thousand and thirty guests.

The tables, spread right and left, were ordered with due discrimination. At the first were seated the kings of Christendom, an English, a Lombard, and a Breton to wit, Otho, Desiderius, and Salomon : and next these all others, according to their dignity and the esteem in which they were held. At the second table were placed the dukes and marquisses ; and at the third, the counts and simple knights. Those of the house of Maganza were especially honoured, and above all the others, Gano of Poictiers. Rinaldo saw this with eyes of fire; the more so that these traitors, laughing amongst themselves, were mocking him as not equally distinguished by the king. Accordingly we are told:

Yet while his heart with smothered fury beats,
He feigns to trifle with the cups and glasses :
But, inly murmuring, to himself repeats
"False, ribald crew ! before to-morrow passes,
"This arm shall prove if you can keep your seats;
"Spawn of a nest of vipers, idiots, asses !
"And well I wot to have you on the hip,
"Unless my weapon swerve, or courser slip."
King Balugantes marked his discontent,
And reading, as he weened, his secret thought,
To him his trucheman with a message sent,
To wot if it was true, as he was taught,
That honour, not by worth and wisdom went,
But in this Christian court was sold and bought :
That he a stranger and a Turk, if true,
Might render each and all the honour due.
The good Ilinaldo smiled, and to the sable
Reporter of the royal message said,
"To solve the question, as I best am able,
"(If I in rules of court am rightly read,)
"Honour and place to glutton at the table
"Are duly yielded, as to dame in bed;
"But in the field, where warriors spur their steeds,
"The worth of man is measured by his deeds."

While this conversation is passing, music sounds; the meats are served up, and the feast is commenced with all the pomp and circumstance of chivalric magnificence.

In the middle of this their merriment, four giants enter the further end of the hall, having between them a damsel of incomparable beauty, attended by a single knight. Many ladies (some of whose names are specified) were seated at the different tables : but all were outshone by the beautiful stranger. The Christians, lords or simple knights, swarm about the damsel, and every Pagan is in an instant on his feet. She smiles upon all; but forthwith addresses herself to Charlemagne. After a complimentary preface, "Sir King," said the damsel, " before I show the motive which has brought us hither, learn that this knight is my brother Uberto, and that I am his sister, Angelica; both of us banished without reason from the paternal mansion. Upon the Tanais, where we dwelt, two hundred days' journey from hence, news were brought us of this feast ; and we have traversed so many provinces to see your magnificence, and, if possible, to gain the wreath of roses, which is said to be the guerdon of the jousts.

"For this purpose, my brother awaits all comers, Christian or Saracen, at the stair of Merlin[14]; it being premised that the war is to be conducted on the following conditions : Whoever is unseated in the tilt, shall be allowed no further course or trial, but remain the prisoner of him by whom he was unhorsed: while whoever flings my brother shall have me for his reward; and Uberto shall depart with his giants."

She remains kneeling awhile before Charles, as waiting his answer. All behold the damsel in mute admiration; but, above all, Orlando, approaching her with downcast eyes, gives the first signs of the passion which was destined to be his ruin. While Orlando is thus love-stricken, he is not single in his folly; and even the

---

[14] It may be observed, that the abode of Merlin and the tomb of Merlin are always placed by the first romancers, to wit, those of the Round Table, in Britain; and their constantly laying their scene in our island, and choosing their actors from thence, has led M. de la Rue, and after him, Mr. George Ellis, to suppose that these earliest romancers were subjects of English kings, who wrote for the amusement of their court, the language of which was Norman. The romancers, however, who celebrated Charlemagne, and who were doubtless French, very naturally chose their heroes from France, and transferred the scene to that country. To these, I have already said, that Boiardo and Ariosto are mainly indebted for their fictions.

grey-haired Namus, and Charles himself, participate in it. But, while these and all the rest gaze upon her in silence, Ferrau is so transported with passion as to be about to snatch her up in his arms, and transport her away from the presence. Respect for Charlemagne, however, restrains him. While this is passing, Malagigi, brother to Rinaldo, a puissant magician, closely observes the strangers, and reads in them some mysterious purpose, different from what they pretended to be the object of their expedition. Charlemagne had now recovered from his embarrassment sufficiently to speak, and plied Angelica with different subjects of discourse, for the purpose of detaining her; but at length, not being able to prolong the interview with decency, gave her a dismissal by according the request

The damsel has scarce left the city, when Malagigi
Still fearing for the king, and full of care,
Flies to his book, retiring from the revel,
To know the secret purpose of the pair,
And at what aim the knight and damsel level.
He reads; and, as he reads, in upper air
Is heard a voice, and next appears a devil,
Who bids, in haughty tone, the wise magician
Proclaim his will, and give him his dismission.

Malagigi having proposed his questions, the fiend informs him that Angelica is an enemy come to put a notable scorn upon Charlemagne, and that her father, who is an ancient Indian king, called Galaphron, of Catay, has dispatched her for this object, accompanied by her brother, Argalia, and not Uberto, as she falsely designated him : that she is full of malice, and read in every sort of magic, whilst her brother is as valiant in arms, gifted with a courser of marvellous swiftness, and armed with an enchanted lance : the virtue of this is such, that no knight (no, not even Orlando or Rinaldo) could resist its push; nor are his other arms inferior to his spear. To this; he has received from his father a ring, which, when on the finger, makes enchantment of no effect, and when placed between the lips renders the wearer invisible. Galaphron, it is added, reckons much upon these gifts, but yet more upon the beauty of his daughter. Hence he has dispatched Argalia with the damsel, in trust, that she shall entice the Paladins into duel with her brother, who, unhorsing them, will send them prisoners to Catay. Malagigi is much disturbed at the devil's news, and determines to seek the damsel in person, and frustrate her design. Argalia was already reposing himself under a fair pavilion, pitched near the stair of Merlin, while

> Angelica beneath a pine was sleeping,
> Her long light tresses scattered on the grass,
> Beside a limpid font, whose waters, leaping,
> Fell back into a pool as clear as glass.
> A giant had the damsel in his keeping,
> Who might for a reposing angel pass.
> Her brother's ring the sleeping lady wore,
> Whose hidden virtues were described before.
> False Malagigi, borne on fiendish steed,
> Meantime through fields of air in silence swept;
> And now, dismounting on the flow'ry mead,
> Approached the weary damsel where she slept,
> By that grim giant watched, who, for her need,
> Good guard upon the sleeping lady kept,
> While others of her following paced the sward,
> And (such their charge) kept wider watch and ward.

The necromancer smiles at seeing the whole party, as it were, delivered over into his hands, and opens his books for the purpose of beginning his operations. Whilst he reads, a heavy slumber falls upon the watchers; and, having drawn his sword, (for he was a belted knight,) he approaches the princess with the intention of putting her to death. He yields, however, to the enchantment of beauty, and determines to make a different use of the opportunity. Not aware that the enchanted ring was on her finger, which she had accidentally received from Argalia, he conceives he has rendered her sleep as fast as that of her followers, and clasps her in his arms; but the ring, which is proof against all spells, does its duty. Angelica wakes with a shriek, and Argalia rushes to her assistance. Being unprovided with other weapon, he avenges the insult offered to his sister with a cudgel; but as he is bruising the unfortunate Malagigi, Angelica cries to him to bind the ravisher fast, while she holds him; as he is a potent necromancer, who, but for the assistance of the ring, would laugh at chains. Argalia runs immediately to wake the giant, but finding, after some time, that this was a fruitless attempt, he himself binds Malagigi, hands and feet. The damsel this while possesses herself of the magician's book, and having evoked his fiends, bids them convey her prisoner instantly to King Galaphron, and inform him that her project goes well, since she has mastered the only enemy whom she had reason to fear. Malagigi is confined by Galaphron, in a dungeon under the sea. In the mean time, Angelica dissolves the enchanted sleep of her followers.

While these things are going on, all is uproar at Paris, since Orlando insists upon being the first to try the adventure at the stair of Merlin. This is resented by the other pretenders to Angelica, and all contest his right to the precedency. The tumult is stilled by the usual expedient of casting lots, and the first prize is drawn by Astolpho. Ferrau has the second, and the giant Grandonio the third. Next to these came Berlinghier and Otho, then Charles himself, and (as his ill fortune would have it), after thirty more, the indignant Orlando.

The character of the holder of the first lot is now developed, who is to play a considerable part in the romance.

Astolpho, who the winning ticket bore,
Was nimble, and with youthful beauty blest;
And, for these gentle gifts, was prized before
Christian or Pagan princes, east or west;
With that, was rich, and full of courteous lore,
And always loved to go in gilded vest !
One only fault the prince's pride might humble;
Sir Turpin tells us he was given to tumble.

Astolpho goes forth upon his adventure with great gaiety of dress and manner, and Argalia and he encounter, after having with much courtesy renewed the engagements, which were before specified as regulating the duel. They engage; when Astolpho is immediately tilted out of his saddle. His rage and surprise are excessive; but his painful feelings receive some relief from the kindness of Angelica, who, moved to compassion for his misfortune, and somewhat touched by his gallantry and grace, grants him the liberty of the pavilion; where he is treated with every sort of kindness and respect. Here he is assigned a magnificent bed; the others retreat to their couches, and thus passes the night.

The sleepers are awakened at dawn by Ferrau's bugle, who, as next upon the list, claims the second course. Argalia goes forth to meet him, clad in his enchanted arms, and mounted on his horse Rabican, who is described as blacker than a crow, save that three of his legs were pie-balled, and that his forehead was marked with a star.

Ferrau undergoes the fate of Astolpho; but when unhorsed, refuses to abide, like him, the established conditions, and springing upon his feet, in despite of the protest of Argalia, renews the battle with his sword. Argalia's giants now rush between the combatants, and attack him; their master, however, in courtesy, retires from such unequal fray, and stands apart till his giants are overthrown. He then renews the contest, and Astolpho, who had been waked by the disturbance, in vain seeks to allay it. Ferrau says that he is no vassal of Charles's, and therefore is not bound by any pact respecting the duel, which he may have made with Angelica : and that he is resolved to win her and wear her. In answer to the observation of Argalia, that he is without a helmet, which had been beat off and broken by the golden lance, he observes, that without one, he is a fair match for his opposite.

This dispute had been carried on by the combatants on foot, but they now remount in order to decide it on horseback, when Argalia in his fury forgets his lance, which he has left leaning against a pine. Many blows had been given and taken without effect, when the two knights paused in mutual astonishment, and Argalia informed Ferrau that his efforts were fruitless, as his armour was enchanted; a communication which Ferrau repaid by observing that his skin was invulnerable with the exception of one

38

side. The recital of these gifts, which produces a sort of reciprocal respect, leads them to a further parley; in which Argalia agrees to give Ferrau Angelica to wife, provided she consents to the arrangement. But Angelica, who is startled by Ferrau's ugliness and fierceness, and more especially by his ill-shaped head and black hair, her favour being especially set upon a light-haired lover, entreats her brother, rather than sacrifice her to such a man, to renew his battle which had been suspended, while she transports herself by magic to Catay; she then observes he may watch his opportunity, to escape and follow her to the wood of Arden, where she will wait his arrival.

He, in consequence, communicates to Ferrau the refusal of his sister. The battle is renewed; and upon its renewal, Angelica disappears. She is soon followed by Argalia, who turns his back upon his adversary. Ferrau pursues, but sees no traces either of the damsel or the knight. In the meantime Astolpho, who finds himself at liberty, puts on his armour, and his own lance having been splintered in the joust, takes, unconscious of its virtues, that of Argalia, which was left leaning against the pine. Returning home, he meets Rinaldo, who had wandered out to the wood, to learn the fortune of Ferrau. He, too, hearing of the disappearance of Angelica, gallops away in pursuit, while Astolpho continues his road to Paris.

Here Orlando seeks him, and learns all that has passed. Distracted with the news, and, above all, jealous of Rinaldo, he too, waits, only till evening to join in the pursuit; when he makes his secret sally, and rides towards the wood of Arden. Thus, three champions, to wit, Ferrau, Rinaldo, and Orlando are entered in the chase.

This, while Charlemagne is proceeding in his preparations for the tournament, the prize of which was to be the Crown of Roses. Many fair feats had already been wrought, and the knights are in the heat of the jousts, when Astolpho pricks forth into the medley[15]; but his courser falls with him and dislocates his foot. All regret this accident of the English prince, who is carried to his

---

[15] Mischia, melee.

palace where his foot is set. The jousts are continued by the others, from whom Grandonio the giant bears — away the honours of the field, wounding and unhorsing knights on all sides. In the meantime,

Astolpho was return'd into the square,
His single faulchion to his girdle tied,
And rode in gallant guise an ambling mare,
Unarm'd and weaponless in all beside :
And laugh'd and loiter'd with the ladies there,
And jested with the circle far and wide :
While he thus idly chatted, Gryphon fell,
Thrust by Grandonio from his lofty sell.

All who contend with Grandonio suffer the same destiny; while the outrageous Pagan overwhelms Charles and his paladins with invective. On the other hand, Charles vents threats and imprecations upon the absent Orlando, Rinaldo, and Gano, expressing at the same time his earnest desire to be revenged upon the Saracens.

Astolpho, hearing this, retreats, unobserved, to his palace, arms himself at all points and reappears amongst the combatants; not, as the author observes, that he expects to do himself much honour; in which opinion he seems to have agreed with the multitude who hailed his entrance with smiles and whispers, but with the intention of doing his duty to his lord, and leaving the event to Heaven. Accordingly

Firm on his prancing steed, he louted low
In graceful act, and " Know, Sir King," he cried,
"I come to venge thee of thy Pagan foe,
"Knowing that thou such wish hast signified."
As one whose mood was still fastidious; " Go,
"Go in the name of God;" King Charles replied :
Then, turning to the lords that hemm'd his seat;
"There lack'd but this to make our shame complete."

Astolpho, thus dismissed, pours a volley of abuse upon Grandonio, and tilts at him in fury. The golden lance works an unexpected miracle, and the giant tumbles like a tower that is undermined. King Charlemagne and all are in amazement, while Astolpho, though no less surprized at his own prowess, pursues his fortune, and clears the field. These events were immediately recounted to Gan, who was in his own house, and who, having armed a party of his kinsmen and retainers, comes before the king, and alleges some frivolous pretext for his tardy appearance; which, whether believed or not, is accepted by the sovereign. He now sends a message to Astolpho, proposing to close the tournament, as the paynims are defeated. To which the English prince replies, ' that he considers him every whit as false a Pagan as the others,' and immediately attacks him with his lance. Gan, Pinabello and all their household are unhorsed; but while Astolpho is in full career, a traitor assails him from behind, and bears him to the ground. He rises in fury, tilts at friends and foes, and outrages all, king Charlemagne among the rest; by whose order he is at last surrounded, mastered, and carried off to prison.

He was here ill bested, yet not so ill, says the
author, as the other three, who suffered the
pains of love for Angelica. These all arrived
by different roads, and at different times in the
wood of Arden. The first comer was Rinaldo;
who, penetrating into the forest, beheld a beautiful fountain
in the shade.

The alabaster vase was wrought with gold,
And the white ground o'erlaid with curious care;
While he who look'd within it, might behold
Green grove, and flowers, and meadow, pictur'd there.
Wise Merlin made it, it is said, of old,
For Tristan when he sigh'd for Yseult fair :
That drinking of its wave, he might forego
The peerless damsel, and forget his woe.
But he to his misfortune never found
That fountain, built beneath the green — wood tree;
Altho' the warrior pac'd a weary round.
Encompassing the world by land and sea.
The waves which in the magic bason bound,

41

Make him unlove who loves. Nor only he
Foregoes his former love; but that, which late
Was his chief pride and pleasure, has in hate.
Mount Alban's lord, whose strength and spirits sink,
For yet the sun was high and passing hot,
Stood gazing on the pearly fountain's brink,
Rapt with the sight of that delicious spot.
At length he can no more; but stoops to drink,
And thirst and love are in the draught forgot :
For such the virtue those cold streams impart,
Changed in an instant is the warrior's heart.
Him, with that forest's wonders unacquainted,
Some paces to a second water bring,
Of chrystal wave with rain or soil untainted.
With all the flowers that wreathe the brows of spring
Kind nature had the verdant margin painted :
And there a pine and beech and olive fling
Their boughs above the stream, and form a bower,
A grateful shelter from the noontide hour.
This was the stream of love, upon whose shore
He chanced, where Merlin no enchantments shed;
But nature here, unchanged by magic lore,
The fountain with such sovereign virtue fed,
That all who tasted loved : whence many, sore
Lamenting their mistake, were ill-bested.
Rinaldo wandered to this water's brink,
But, sated, had no further wish to drink.
Yet the delicious trees and banks produce
Desire to try the grateful shade; and needing
Repose, he 'lights, and turns his courser loose,
Who roam'd the forest, at his pleasure feeding;
And there Rinaldo cast him down, at truce
With care; and slumber to repose succeeding,
Thus slept supine : when spiteful fortune brought
Her[16] to the spot whom least the warrior sought.

---

[16] Angelica.

She thirsts, and lightly leaping from her steed,
Ties the gay palfrey to the lofty pine;
Then plucking from the stream a little reed,
Sips, as a man might savour muscat wine;
And feels while yet she drinks (such marvel breed
The waters fraught with properties divine)
She is no longer what she was before;
And next beholds the sleeper on the shore.

Enamoured of the slumbering knight, she hesitates long between love and shame, but, at length, no longer mistress of herself, pulls a handful of flowers, and flings them in his face. The gallantry is lost upon Rinaldo; who wakes, and flies from her with loathing. She pursues, and entreats his compassion in vain; and, at length, wearied with the chace, sinks down upon the turf, and weeps herself asleep. Ferrau now arrives in the forest, in the hope of finding Angelica, or wreaking his vengeance upon her brother. Occupied with these thoughts he lights upon Argalia; who, having followed his sister, had dismounted, and was also sleeping under a tree. Ferrau unties the sleeper's horse, and drives him into the thicket. His adversary's means of escape thus intercepted, he watches till the sleeping man should wake; nor is his patience put to a long trial. Argalia soon opens his eyes, and is in great distress at finding his horse gone; but Ferrau, who is as quickly on his feet, tells him not to think of his loss; as one of them must not quit the place alive, and his own horse will remain the prize of the survivor.

The two warriors now again engage in battle, and closing, Ferrau, through a chink in his armour, strikes Argalia to the heart. Argalia sinks beneath the blow, and dying entreats his adversary to have regard to his honor, and cast him and his armour into the river; that his memory may not be disgraced by the knowledge of his having been vanquished in enchanted arms. Ferrau, who compassionates his fate, promises compliance, with the reservation of wearing his helmet till he can provide himself with another. Argalia consents by a sign, and soon after expires.

Ferrau, who had waited by him till he drew his last sigh, now puts on the helmet, which he had previously taken from his wounded adversary's head in order to give him air; and having razed off the crest, places it upon his own. He then, with the dead body under his arm, having remounted his horse, proceeds sadly towards the neighbouring river, into which he casts Argalia, all armed as he was, conformably to his dying request. He then pursues his melancholy way through the wood.

This while Orlando had arrived on this theatre of adventures, and comes suddenly upon Angelica, who is described as sleeping in act so exquisitely graceful, that he gazes on the vision hi stupid wonderment, and, at last, to contemplate her more closely, throws himself down by her side.

Ferrau arrives at this juncture, and supposing Orlando, whom he had not recognized, to be Angelica's guard, insults and defies him. The paladin starts up and declares himself; when Ferrau, though somewhat surprized, making a virtue of necessity, stands to his arms. A desperate duel follows : during this Angelica wakes and flies : Orlando proposes a truce to his adversary, that he may follow her; but Ferrau, whose courage was now up, tells him she shall be the prize of the conqueror, and refuses. The battle is therefore renewed with more fury than before. The author here exclaims :

Gifted with odd half lights, I often wonder
How I should think of love; if well or ill.
For whether 'tis a thing above, or under
The rule of reason, foils my little skill;
If we go guided by some god, or blunder
Into the snare, which warps our better will;
If we by line and rule our actions measure,
And 'tis a thing we take or leave at pleasure.
When we behold two bulls each other tear,
A cow the cause of strife, with mutual wound,
It looks as if such foolish fury were
In nature and controlling instinct found :
But when we see that absence, prudence, care

44

And occupation, can preserve us sound
From such a charm, or, if you will, infection;
Love seems to be the fruit of pure election.
Of this so many men have sung and told,
In Hebrew, Latin, and in heathen Greek,
In Egypt, Athens, and in Rome, of old,
Who govern'd by such different judgments speak,
That I can ill decide with whom to hold,
And cannot waste my time the truth to seek.
Let it suffice, that Love's a wayward god :
And so heav'n keep us from the tyrant's rod !

The truth of these reflections the author considers as strikingly exemplified by the combat between the champions, which is interrupted by the appearance of a strange damsel upon a panting palfrey, who clamours eagerly for Ferrau. She, perceiving him, entreats Orlando to forbear his blows; which he immediately does upon the damsel's request. Addressing herself to the paynim, she informs him that she is his relation Flordespina, and dispatched in search of him, to say that Gradasso king of Sericane, a fiend incarnate, has invaded the Spanish dominions; that king Falsiron is taken, Valencia ravaged, Arragon destroyed, and Barcelona besieged; that poor Marsilius is broken down by so many calamities, and that his last hopes rest on him, in pursuit of whom she was wandering. Ferrau balances for a moment between love and duty, but at length determines to suspend his combat, with the permission of Orlando, who agrees to the proposal, and who himself follows Angelica. Ferrau, on the other hand, departs with Flordespina for Spain. The author here leaves each to pursue his separate quest, and returns to Charles. This monarch calls a council in consequence of intelligence received, which was similar to that brought by Flordespina to Ferrau. He observes in this council, that Marsilius is his neighbour and relation, and is yet more entitled to succour from a consideration of common danger; and in consequence, with the consent of his peers, dispatches Rinaldo with a great charge of men at arms against Gradasso, who had crossed the streights of Gibraltar into Spain. He at the same time constitutes Rinaldo lieutenant of his southern provinces, who departs for the seat of war; and all the knights present at the tournament assemble under his banner. His coming, as well as that of Ferrau, (now arrived) is highly gratifying to Marsilius, who had sheltered himself in Gerona. The greatest part of Spain (as stated) had been already sacked, and all the Spanish warriors (with the exception of Ferrau) who had returned to the defence of their country, were killed, or prisoners. Even the giant-king, Grandonio, who we lately saw braving Charlemagne and all his peerage, had sought refuge in Barcelona. Marsilius, on the arrival of the French succours, now marches to his relief. The banners of the allied army are no sooner distinguished by Gradasso, where he lay camped, and served by giant-kings, than he issues extravagant orders to his various vassals. Four of these he dispatches with their followers against Barcelona, with orders not leave a soul alive in that city, with the exception of Grandonio, whom he wishes (as he says) to take alive, that he may bait him with his dogs. Others are sent forth, with orders to take or destroy the most distinguished amongst the captains of the confederates. This last command is given to Faraldo, king of Arabia, who is enjoined to bring him Rinaldo and the banner of Charlemagne, which, it seems, was also one of the principal objects of his expedition.

The battle now rages in the field, and within the city of Barcelona, in which the army of Gradasso had previously made lodgements. While the warfare within the town is still doubtful, the bands dispatched against the confederates under Rinaldo, are, after a long contest, defeated; and one of the surviving giantkings reports their discomfiture to Gradasso, who immediately arms and goes forth against the conquerors. His first object of attack is Rinaldo; but Bayardo, startled by the appearance of the Alfana, a monstrous mare, on which Gradasso rode, made a leap of twenty feet into the air, and thus evaded the charge. Gradasso, though somewhat surprized, gallops on, and unhorses many of the best amongst the confederates, who are immediately taken and bound by Alfrera, one of his giant-kings, who serves him as a lacquey.

Rinaldo now wheels Bayardo round, and spurs him at Gradasso; and both charge with such fury, that the Alfana and Bayardo crumble under their riders, who, however, preserve then" seats. Gradasso, who first recollects himself, gives immediate orders to Alfrera, who was following him upon a camelopard, to secure Rinaldo and his horse; and according to his practice, himself follows up the pursuit of the confederates.

Alfrera has, however, a more difficult task assigned him than Gradasso had imagined; for Bayardo, having regained his feet, bears away his rider, who was not yet himself. The paladin, however, waking from his short stupor, rides again hi chase of Gradasso, himself pursued in vain by the giant Alfrera.

Rinaldo charges Gradasso just as he has unhorsed his brother Alardo, and discharges a furious stroke upon his head. Gradasso repays the greeting in a way that would have ended the strife, but for Mambrino's helmet, which saved the knight from any worse evil than a concussion of the brain; while Bayardo again galloped away with him in a state of half stupefaction. Recovering himself a second time, and full of shame and fury, he returns to seek Gradasso, and the combat is renewed with more equality than was promised by its commencement; Rinaldo, counterbalancing the strength of his opposite, by his own superior dexterity, and the quickness and docility of Bayardo. The combatants are, however, separated, and borne asunder by the tide of battle. After different adventures, they yet again meet, when Gradasso observing that Rinaldo is surrounded by the troops of Sericane, courteously proposes that their duel should be deferred till the succeeding day, to be fought under the following conditions, by both combatants on foot : " If Rinaldo conquers, he is to have back all the prisoners made by Gradasso; and if Gradasso wins the day, he is to have Bayardo for his prize; but is in either case to return home, and never more set foot in Europe." Rinaldo willingly accedes to this, and a place is fixed on, near the sea, for the combat, to which both are to come, with no other than defensive armour and their swords. But the author, while the barriers are preparing, returns to Angelica, who, being returned to India, determines on setting Malagigi at liberty, and making him her mediator with the disdainful knight. She accordingly frees him from his dungeon, unlocks his fetters with her own hand, and bids him hi return to unloosen her own. She then returns him his book, explains herself more precisely, and promises him final liberty, on condition of his bringing back Rinaldo.

Malagigi calls up a demon with the aid of his book, mounts him and departs. He is entertained, during his journey, with a relation of Gradasso's enterprise, by the devil; who told him, as the author observes, " all that had chanced, and indeed more, which was so much the easier, in that he lied." Malagigi arrived at his destination, finds Rinaldo rejoiced to see him, but immoveable on the subject of Angelica; and hence, after many fruitless endeavours, vanishes with a threat. Having reached a spot convenient for his incantations, he opens his book, calls up a legion of demons, and from these, selects Draghinazzo and Falsetta. The latter is — bid to take the appearance of one of king Marsilius's heralds, the coat of arms and battoon; and thus equipped, to inform Gradasso that Rinaldo expects to meet him at mid-day. Gradasso accepts the invitation, and gifts the false herald with a cup.

The same devil, again transformed, comes now to Rinaldo, as if from Gradasso, but with a very different appearance. He has a turban on his head, wears a flowing robe, and has rings in his ears, instead of on his fingers. His object is to remind Rinaldo, on the part of Gradasso, to meet him in the morning, which had been the time previously stipulated. Thus each, on the supposed invitation of the other, prepares for a different appointment. Rinaldo necessarily is first at the place, but sees nothing but a

Small pinnace anchor'd by the shore.

He, however, immediately after, descries a figure on the beach, in the garb and guise of Gradasso, but which was, in reality, no other than one of the fiends, Draghinazzo, evoked by Malagigi, and thus transmogrified. The combat immediately begins; and Rinaldo, after some blows given and taken, making a desperate two-handed stroke at the supposed Gradasso, buries his sword Fusberta in the sand. The devil avails himself of the opportunity to escape, flies to the boat, and is putting off. Rinaldo, however, follows him into his barque, and deals a blow at him, but the demon leaps from prow to poop :

Rinaldo chas'd him back from poop to prow,
The sword Fusberta flaming in his hand;
But he from side to side, from stern to bow,
Flits, while the barque is drifting from the land.
Rinaldo marks it not; who thought but how
To reach the foe with his avenging brand;
Nor from his long day-dream of vengeance woke,
Till the false fiend was melted into smoke.

Yet the paladin will not give over his hopes of finding him, and renews a fruitless search above and below. In the meantime, the barque is seven miles from shore, and Rinaldo observes, too late, that she is scudding, self-steered, before the wind.

The vessel at length takes the ground near a beautiful garden, and Rinaldo lands in front of a palace, worthy of its grounds. Here, says the author, I leave him, with less compunction, as he is in good quarters, and proceed in pursuit of Orlando, who, having wandered as far as the Tanais, in search of Angelica, meets an old man weeping the loss of his son, who had been taken prisoner by a giant. The paladin delivers the youth, and the old man, in gratitude, presents him with a book, which is capable (he says) of resolving the questions of any one who consults it. Instructed by this book, he seeks a sphynx, who appears to have been a yet better resolver of doubts, hi order to obtain information of the dwelling-place of Angelica. The monster tells him, that this is in Albracca of Catay. In the meantime the sphinx has her question for the interrogator, which it is death not to interpret; and plies Orlando with the riddle, solved by Œdipus. Orlando, with intent to cut the knot which he cannot untie, draws Durindana, attacks the monster sword in hand, and at length slays and tumbles her from the rock on which she made her abode. He has now leisure to look in his book for the solution of the sphynx's enigma; and finds that her question of " What animal "begins his career upon four legs, after a time "continues it on two, and ends it upon three ?" means Man; designating thus the child who crawls, the man who walks, and the old man who supports himself with a stick. Having cleared up this point, he pursues his way still poring upon the book, and soon arrives at a river dark, deep, and dangerous, whose precipitous banks afford no means of passage. Orlando rides along the shore till he comes to a bridge, where he dismounts. This is kept by a giant, who tells him that he who arrives at that bridge, which is justly named the Bridge of Death, has little while to live; for that all the roads which lead from it wind back to that fatal water, into which either he or Orlando must soon be plunged never to rise again. Orlando, however, who seems little impressed by this warning, springs upon the bridge, and attacks him. A desperate combat now ensues, but with the usual issue. The giant is slain. He, however, in falling, springs a clap-net of iron, which closing on the paladin, beats his sword out of his hand, and envelopes him in its folds.

As he lies helpless in this trap, a friar arrives, who, after vain attempts to release him, offers him spiritual consolation, which is ill received : but the friar, having the sinner at his mercy, continues to inculcate it; and in illustration of the powers of a protecting Providence informs him of a late miraculous escape of his own. He was travelling with certain of his brothers, when they were surprised by a horrible cyclops, who made a feast on one of his companions, but cast him from a rock, as worthless carrion; when he luckily lighted amongst the branches of a tree, where he lay concealed till evening, and then effected his escape. He is yet engaged in his narration, when he breaks off with a scream and flies.

His sudden terror was produced by the sight of the very Cyclops of whom he spoke, who came armed with a club and three darts. He, however, instead of pursuing the friar, stops to consider Orlando. He then takes up Durindana, which lies near, and hews the chain-net in pieces, without injury to the count, whose skin was enchanted. Orlando instantly starts up, his bones aching with the blows, which had not been able to penetrate his flesh; and seizing the giant's club, they, having thus exchanged weapons, engage in a desperate and equal combat. For if Orlando's skin was invulnerable, the giant's armour, which was made of griffins' claws, was equally impenetrable. At length Orlando bethinks him of the three shafts, which the giant had laid down, as well as his club, when he possessed himself of Durindana.

Seizing these, and launching one of them at his single eye, it penetrates his brain and stretches him dead. At this juncture the friar, who yet trembles with fear as well as joy, reappears, and entreats Orlando to accompany him towards the dead cyclops' den, for the purpose of liberating his companions.

This done, Orlando rides on; when, arriving at a place where many roads cross, he meets a courier, and asking him news, learns that he is dispatched by Angelica, to solicit the aid of Sacripant, king of Circassia, in favour of her father, Galaphron, besieged by Agrican, emperor of Tartary, in Albracca. This Agrican had been an unsuccessful suitor to the damsel, whom he now pursues with arms. Orlando, who learns that he is within a day's journey of Albracca, now thinks that he is secure of Angelica, and proceeds with rapture towards her seat.

Thus journeying, he arrives at a bridge which united two mountains, and under which ran a foaming river. Here a damsel meets him with a goblet, and informs him, with much grace of demeanor, that it is the usage of the bridge to present the traveller with a cup, which she offers to Orlando, and which the paladin, in courtesy, drains. He has, however, no sooner swallowed the julep which sparkles in it, than his brain dances, and he is no longer conscious of the object of his journey, or even of his own existence. Under the influence of this fascination, he follows the damsel into a magnificent and marvellous palace.

Here the author leaves the count to return to Gradasso, who, deceived by the false herald that appointed him to meet Rinaldo upon the sea-shore at noon, in vain expects his arrival. He waits there till night, when he retires full of indignation at the supposed cowardice of his opponent. In the meantime, Ricciardetto (who had been left by his brother, Rinaldo, in charge of Charlemagne's army), on the paladin's departure for the false appointment according to the instructions he had received, in case of his not returning in a given time, withdraws Charles's forces from Marsilius's camp, and returns to France.

Gano immediately cries out upon Rinaldo's treason, and all is dismay. On the other part, Marsilius, thus deserted, has no means of safety, but in making peace with Gradasso, and consenting to hold Spain as his liegeman. In consequence of his so doing, Gradasso, strengthened by the accession of Marsilius, with Grandonio and his other vassal kings, marches upon Paris. Charlemagne, with all his peerage, sallies to encounter him; but his army experiences a disastrous rout, and he, with almost all his paladins, is captured; while Paris is immediately invested by the invaders.

Gradasso, however, does not abuse his victory : he takes Charles by the hand, seats him by his side, and tells him he wars only for honour. Hence he renounces all conquests, but insists on the monarch promising him Bayardo and Durindana, both the property of his vassals, the first of which, as he maintained, was already forfeited by the treason of Rinaldo. To this; Charlemagne and his peers in acknowledgment of their defeat, were to remain his prisoners for a day : Bayardo, who had been brought back by Ricciardetto, was to be forthwith delivered up, and Durindana consigned to Gradasso in Sericana, upon the return of Orlando to France. To these terms Charlemagne readily accedes, and sends for the horse to Paris.

Here, Astolpho had assumed the command, having obtained his freedom during the confusion, which followed upon the rout of Charlemagne's army, and asserted an authority which, in the absence of the other peers, there was no one to dispute.

He receives with great indignation the messenger dispatched for Bayardo, and throws him into prison; answering the embassy by a herald, who says, on the part of Astolpho, "that Charles has no right in the steed; but that Gradasso may come and fight for him; in which case he will meet him in the field."

The next day the two knights encounter, having previously established the conditions of their combat. The enchanted lance performs a new wonder; and Gradasso, the terrible Gradasso, is unhorsed.

According to their previous agreement, Gradasso is to give up his prisoners, and return to his kingdom of Sericana. Astolpho, however, begs him not to spoil a jest which he wishes to put upon Charlemagne and his paladins, by making them believe that the issue of the duel had been different from what it was, and that they, therefore, (in consequence of the first proffer of Gradasso not having been acceded to,) were still the prisoners of that sovereign. When Astolpho has sufficiently bantered both king, count, and bishop (for Turpin was amongst the captives, and one of the objects of his raillery), he falls upon his knees, begs pardon of Charles for his irreverence, and observes, that as he is ill looked upon in his court, he will leave the field to Gano, and set out on the morrow in search of his cousins Orlando and Rinaldo. Having said this, Charles and his peers are freed, and Gano is getting into his saddle; when he is brought back by Astolpho, who observes, that he only gives him his liberty, (since the disposal of all is at his option,) on condition of his swearing before Charles, to constitute himself his prisoner for four days, whenever he should enjoin it. Charles undertakes for his compliance with such a requisition, and seeks to detain Astolpho with the bribe of Ireland; but the duke is inflexible, and departs. Gradasso also returns into Sericana.

The author now returns to Rinaldo, who was landed by the self-piloted boat in what was, it seems, denominated The Joyous Garden. He is scarcely disembarked, before a lady appears, who takes him by the hand, and conducts him into a palace, where he is served by attendant damsels, with everj r sort of luxury and magnificence. At last, the chief of the servants tells him, that all this is his which he surveys, being the present of a lady, who, to have his love, has brought him out of Spain. While Rinaldo stands lost in astonishment, the name of Angelica, who is proclaimed by this man to be the mistress of the palace, breaks the charm, and he flies in fury through the garden, till, arriving at the landing-place, he leaps again into his pinnace. The bark, however, remains immoveable, and he is about to cast himself into the sea in despair, when it darts from the shore and traverses the waves.

Arrived on the banks of a well-wooded country, it again takes the land; and Rinaldo disembarking, encounters a hoary and aged man upon the beach, who has a melancholy story for the paladin, of a ravisher who had that moment carried away his daughter. Pursuing the thief, Rinaldo falls into a pit-fall, and is carried away prisoner by a giant; who bears him to a castle, situated upon a promontory, the walls of which were covered with maimed bodies and heads, some of which yet quivered with the remains of life.

The giant, entering the building, casts Rinaldo down before an old woman of stern and forbidding appearance; who thus addresses him:

"Haply, Sir Knight, thou hast not heard display
Our castle's use," exclaims the beldame old;
In the short time thou hast to live, a day
Is yet thine own, the story shall be told :
Then listen to the legend, whilst thou may,
And I the melancholy tale unfold.
Thou in that space may'st hear the tale of sorrow,
And witness to its truth in blood to-morrow."

She pursues her story[17] thus : "Know, Sir Stranger, that this castle was formerly held by a rich lord, famous for his magnificence and hospitality, and yet more so, for the

---

[17] I have thought it the duty of a translator, to preserve this story; but I would say to my readers, in the words of Ariosto,
Lasciate questo canto, che senz' esso
Puo star l' istoria, e non sara men' chiara.
Mettendolo Turpino, anch' io l' ho messo.
Leave out this canto; since the tale will tell
Without it, and the story is as clear:
Which, told by Turpin, I relate as well.

incomparable beauty of the lady whom he had to wife. This castellan was hight Gryphon, his castle Altaripa, and Stella was the name of his wife. It was his favourite pleasure to disport himself in the green-wood near the shore, where thou arrived'st this morning, and roving one day through this, he heard the hunting-horn of a stranger, whom he invited to his castle. The guest was Marchino, lord of Aronda, and my husband; who was so smitten by the beauty of Stella, that he could not rest till he had made her his own. He, however, dissembled his evil intentions, and took a friendly leave of his entertainer. This was only to return, as a treacherous enemy. He, accordingly, bearing some resemblance to Gryphon, counterfeited his ensigns, and came back with a party of his retainers, whom he concealed, as well as those, in the neighbouring wood. He, in the mean time, pursued the chace unarmed. Gryphon again sought him out, and finding him apparently distressed by the loss of a hound, joined him in his search. He was thus decoyed into the ambuscade, and assassinated. Marchino, having disposed of his rival, entered Altaripa under the disguise of Gryphon's ensigns, where he did not leave a soul alive, with the exception of Stella. She, while preserved by the conqueror, brooded in secret over schemes of vengeance, and after pondering some time, determined to have recourse to that animal whose wrath is the most intolerable, namely, the wife who has been once loved, and after slighted for another. This was no other than myself, and the cruelties which I perpetrated, well justified her expectation. Two children, whom I had by Marchino, I killed and quartered. Think upon this : yet know that I still triumph in the recollection of my vengeance. Their heads only, I preserved: the remainder I cooked, and served up to the wretched father for his supper. This done, I departed secretly for the court of the king of Orgagna, who had long been a wooer to me, without success. Him I stirred up to vengeance against Marchino, and brought in arms against his newlyacquired castle of Altaripa.

While I was gone on this errand, Stella, with dishevelled hair, a smile upon her lips, but bitterness in her heart, presented herself before the murderer of her husband, with the heads of his two children in a charger, and disclosed to him the horrid tragedy, at which he had been an unwitting assistant. The traitor hesitated for a moment, as if suspended between the desire of lust and vengeance, and then slew the lady, and satiated both; nay, as if in outrage of God and man, pursued his impious loves with the body, till I returned with the king of Orgagna.

After a desperate resistance, we possessed ourselves of Altaripa, and Marchino, having been made prisoner, perished in such tortures as he had deserved.

The king of Orgagna now departed, leaving me mistress of the conquered castle, with three giants for my defence, having first buried the unfortunate Stella, together with the body of Gryphon, which had been left exposed and subjected to outrage by the barbarous Marchino.

More than eight months had now passed when a horrid cry was heard from the marble sepulchre, in which Gryphon and Stella were laid, and we fled in dismay from the sound. Only one of my giants, more daring than his fellows, approached the tomb, and lifted the lid; when a monster thrust forth its claw, and having dragged him into the grave, devoured him alive. We immediately walled up the space about the monument, as a protection against its attacks, and the monster, having made its way out of the sepulchre, remains thus enclosed between the defences which we have constructed. But such is his rage and craving for human flesh, that we supply him with this, lest he should tear down the wall in his fury. Hence the usage of this castle; which is to seize on all strangers, in order to provide him with food. The quarters which you see exposed on the walls, are the leavings of the beast: for though the custom sprung out of necessity, my heart is become hardened with cruelty, and I now live for no other pleasure."

Rinaldo hears the hag with stern composure, and desires no other favour than that of being exposed to the monster, clad in armour, as he is, and with Fusberta in his hand. This the beldam grants, with a bitter smile of mockery, and the night closes upon him in his dungeon.

The succeeding morning, he is lowered down from the wall into the space tenanted by the beast, the horrible fruit of Marchino's intercourse with the body of Stella. A desperate combat now ensues, Rinaldo being unable to make any impression on the scales of the monster : while he, on the contrary, shears away plate and mail from the paladin. While he is engaged in this hopeless struggle, the beast seizes Fusberta with his teeth, and disarms Rinaldo, who is left without defence.

The author here leaves him, as he says, to speak of a spirit hardly less afflicted, though in another manner : he means Angelica; who expects in trembling, the effect of Malagigi's attempt. He arrives, and states his failure, but would comfort the damsel with the thoughts of vengeance; relating to what a perilous pass he had brought the miserable Rinaldo; for it was by his stratagem that he was conveyed to Altaripa. She, however, is in despair at his danger, and overwhelms Malagigi with repoaches. He tells her, it is not yet too late to save him, and furnishes her with the means. These are a rope, with a noose at the distance of every palm, a cake of wax, and a file. Furnished with these implements, and instructed by Malagigi in the use of them, Angelica fliesr" through the air to the succour of Rinaldo.

The miserable paladin had, in the mean time, sprang upon a beam, which projected from the wall, and thus remained hanging between heaven and earth, with little hope even of present safety; since the monster continually leapt at him, and, often, all but reached him with his claws. It was now evening, when Rinaldo was surprised by the shadow of a woman, and soon after by the sight of Angelica, kneeling before him, self-suspended in air. She reproaches herself for having brought him into this peril, and opening her arms, entreats him to take refuge in them, and escape. Such, however, are the effects of the fountain of hate, that Rinaldo spurns at the proposal, and vows if she does not immediately depart, he will cast himself down from the beam. After long and fruitless efforts to move him, she at length descends, throws her cake of wax to the monster, and immediately flings her rope, knotted with nooses, before him. The beast, who takes the bait, finding his teeth glued together by the wax, vents his fury in bounds, and leaping into one of the snares is noosed by Angelica, who leaves him thus entangled, and departs.

Though the monster is delivered over to him gagged and bound, so invulnerable is his hide, that Rinaldo makes long and fruitless efforts to destroy him; till, at length, leaping upon his neck, he squeezes his eyes out of their sockets; and the beast expires under the gripe.

Another difficulty yet remained to be overcome. The walls were of immense height, and the only opening in them was a grated window, of such strength that Fusberta was unable to separate the bars. In his distress, however, Rinaldo perceived the file which had been left by Angelica on the ground, and, with the help of this, effected his deliverance.

He is immediately discovered and surrounded, but he charges and slays his pursuers; and the beldam, having witnessed the destruction of her followers, throws herself headlong from a balcony of three hundred feet in height.

Departing hence, Rinaldo returns to the seaside; but, unwilling to trust himself again to the bark, pursues his way along the shore.

The author now returns to Astolpho, who had set out in search of his cousins, Orlando and Rinaldo, splendidly dressed and equipt, as was his use, and mounted on Bayardo; in the intention of returning him to his lord. Having arrived in Circassia, he finds there a great army, encamped under the command of Sacripant, the king of that country; who was leading it to the defence of Galaphron, the father of Angelica. Astolpho visits the camp of this faithful, but ill-requited lover of the princess; and not having the leopard on his buckler, which was of gold, is known through the Circassian army as the knight of the golden shield. Sacripant, much struck by the appearance of Astolpho and his horse, accosts him affably, and

Demands how his assistance may be bought,

And bids him make his price of service known,
"With gift of this fair host, whom thou hast brought
To war in Indian fields from tower and town;"
The British duke replies, "With this, or nought.
Leave me, or make me at this price thine own.
Nor will I serve, sir king, for other pay,
Born to command, unweeting to obey."

This, with other more extravagant speeches, leads the
Circassian captains to consider him as a madman, and Astolpho is
left to pursue his journey. King Sacripant, however, has been too
much struck with the appearance of his horse and armour, to part
with him so easily, and having divested himself of his kingly
ornaments, he determines to pursue him.

Astolpho was in the meantime advanced a day's journey
upon his road, when he was overtaken by a strange warrior :

The stranger knight was named sir Brandimart,
Lord of the Sylvan Tower and its domain :
Through paynim countries, and in every part
Bruited for glorious feats, by hill and plain.
Well versed in tilt and tourney's valiant art;
In his appearance graceful and humane :
Courteous, with that : and over and above
His other virtues, famed for constant love.
A gentle damsel had the knight for guide,
Who with Astolpho bold encountered there;
Blooming in early youth and beauty's pride;
And in his faithful eyes as dear as fair.
Him from afar the British duke[18] defied,
And proudly bade him for the joust prepare
And wheel and take his ground, and guard his right,
"Or leave his lady love, a prize to better knight."

Brandimart is as ready for battle as Astolpho; but observes,
as the latter has no lady, he may wager his horse; as it was but fair
that each should deposit his stake. The proposal is acceded to,

---

[18] Astolpho.

and the knights encounter. Brandimart is unhorsed, and his steed falls dead, while Bayardo remains uninjured by the shock.

The paynim knight observing the disconsolate looks of the damsel, is so overwhelmed with despair, that he draws his sword and is about to plunge it into his own bosom. Astolpho, however, holds his hand, and exclaims that he contended but for glory, and having won the honours of the fight, was contented to leave him the lady.

While Brandimart is vowing eternal service and gratitude, king Sacripant arrives, and now longing for the damsel of the one as well as the steed and arms of the other, defies them to the joust. Astolpho, as mounted, meets the challenger, whom he instantly overthrows, and presents Brandimart with his courser; leaving the king to return to his army on foot. This disposition is scarcely made, when Brandimart's damsel changes colour, and tells them they are approaching the waters of Oblivion, and advises them either to turn back, or to change their direction. Both refuse; and pursuing their path, arrive at the bridge where Orlando was left.

The damsel, as before, appears with the enchanted chalice, which is rejected by Astolpho with contumely. She immediately dashes it to the ground, and a fire blazes up, which renders the bridge impassable. Upon this the damsel, who accompanied them, seizes each by the hand, runs with them along the river, and brings them to another secret and narrow bridge, which they cross in safety, and find themselves beside the enchanted garden.

Brandimart instantly batters down the gate, and the two warriors entering, are attacked by sundry knights known and unknown, who, having no recollection of any thing, join blindly in the defence of their prison-house. While these are engaged by Brandimart, Astolpho entering the garden and pursuing his career, meets with Orlando, who being, like the rest, mindless of kindred or of country, makes at the English duke, who only escapes by the activity of Bayardo. He clears the wall, and bears off his rider.

The author pauses to tell us that the enchanted water signifies the affection, impression, or opinion which man takes from others, either at sight, or upon trust; and the cup, which the damsel lets fall, is that which gives its colouring to the thing seen.

Bayardo, this time, continues to gain upon Orlando's horse; and while Astolpho is thus born out of danger, Brandimart is overlaid with fearful odds in the enchanted garden; and his lady, trembling for the issue of the battle, entreats him to yield to necessity, and comply with the usage of the fairy. So saying, she flies; and Brandimart, obeying her commands, yields, and drinking of the cup, becomes as intoxicated as the rest.

Orlando returns from the fruitless pursuit of Astolpho, and excuses himself to the fairy, who was named Dragontina, for not having been able to overtake her enemy; who pursues his way to Albracca, which Agrican is about to besiege. Here he is welcomed kindly by Angelica, though she is somewhat outraged by his rhodomontades. He is not long before he attempts to put them in practice. For having one night ordered the drawbridge to be lowered, he sallies out alone, arrives in Agrican's camp, and unhorses his warriors, right and left, by means of the enchanted lance. Being, however, surrounded and taken, his capture spreads consternation among the besieged, and the author says that no one dared sally from the city.

Relief, was, however at hand; for, as the burghers and soldiers, are one day, leaning over their walls, they descry a cloud of dust, from which horsemen are seen to prick forth, as it rolls on towards the camp of the besiegers, which lay between the town and the new army that was approaching.

This turns out to be the army of Sacripant, which, arriving the morning after the capture of Astolpho, attacks that of Agrican, with the view of cutting a passage through his camp into the besieged city. Agrican, however, mounted on Bayardo, taken from Astolpho, but not armed with the lance of gold, with the virtues of which he appears to have been unacquainted, performs prodigies, and rallies his scattered troops, which had given way to the sudden and unexpected assault. Sacripant, on the other hand, encourages his own by the most desperate acts of valour, and, as an additional incentive to his courage, sends a messenger to

Angelica, entreating that she will appear upon the walls. She not only complies with this invitation, but sends him a sword as an earnest of her favour.

She arrives in time to see a single combat between the two leaders, Agrican and Sacripant: in this, however, her defender appears to be rather overmatched, when the Circassians break the ring, and separate the two combatants, who are borne asunder by the crowd. Sacripant, who was severely wounded, profits by the occasion, and escapes into Albracca, where he is put to bed and carefully attended.

The duel is an omen of the event of the battle, and the Circassians, who had at first penetrated within their enemies' lines, are now routed and fly in confusion towards the town. Angelica orders the drawbridge to be lowered, and the gates to be thrown open to the fugitives. With these Agrican, who was not distinguished hi the hurly-burly, enters the place pell mell, driving both Circassians and Catayans before him, and the portcullis is instantly dropt.

Thus shut into the besieged city, the Tartar king continues the chase, regardless of his retreat being intercepted, and deluges the streets with blood. Sacripant, hearing the tumult, and learning the cause, leaps from bed, naked and wounded as he was, and armed only with his sword and shield, opposes himself to his fury. His example and his reproaches take effect. Her allies the flyers, and, fresh forces coming to his assistance, and pouring in upon Agrican from all sides, the Tartar king slowly and reluctantly retreats.

The author here suspends this story, to speak ofRinaldo; whom we left issuing from the castle of Altaripa, and pursuing his way along the beach. Here he meets with a weeping damsel, who, being questioned as to the cause of her sorrow, tells him she wanders upon a hopeless quest, and is in search of one who will do battle with nine knights, amongst whom is Orlando. This is the lady loved of Brandimart; to whom Rinaldo promises his assistance, trusting to accomplish the adventure either by valour or by skill. The author here pauses from his narrative, and exclaims,

> To the grim winter and the dismal night
> Succeed the balmy spring and cheerful day.
> That battle had so fill'd me with affright,
> That I was all confusion and dismay :
> But now the strife is over, and 'tis light,
> Of ladies and of love shall be my lay;
> And I will piece my broken tale and tell
> What good Rinaldo and the maid befell.

The damsel, on their setting out together on the adventure, insists upon Rinaldo's taking her horse. This he refuses, and a contest of courtesy follows, which is ended by Rinaldo's accepting the palfrey, on condition of her mounting upon the croup. This she does, in some fear for her honour; but finding the cavalier cold and silent, at last proposes to beguile the way with a story. To this he consents, and she begins her narration as follows:

"There lived of late, in Babylon, a cavalier, called Iroldo, who had for his wife a lady named Tisbina, to whom he was passionately attached. Near them dwelt a Babylonian gentleman, named Prasildo, rich, gay, courteous and valiant; who, making one of a party of both sexes, in a garden, where a game was played which admitted familiarities between them, fell desperately in love with Tisbina, whom he vainly solicited, by every kind of gallantry and magnificence.

"All his efforts were however unavailing; and, disappointed in his hope, he fell into a state of melancholy which rendered life intolerable. One only occupation seemed to afford him some little relief. This was to brood over his sorrows in a wood, situated at a small distance from Babylon.

"As he here one day indulged his grief, (and it grew by indulgence,) he fell into such a fit of passion, that he determined, after a broken soliloquy, to slay himself and die with the name of Tisbina on his lips. By a strange accident, his intention was overheard by Iroldo and Tisbina herself, who were walking

63

together in the wood. They were both moved to compassion; and Iroldo insisted upon Tisbina's offering some consolation to the despairing lover.

"Her husband leaving her, that she may execute this purpose, she comes upon him as if by accident; pretends that, though modesty has hitherto restrained her, she has not been insensible to his tenderness; and assures him, that, if he will give her an indubitable proof of his devotion, in undertaking an adventure which she has at heart, she will reward him with the possession of her person.

"She then tells him that beyond the woods of Barbary, there is a garden, which is surrounded by an iron wall, to be entered through four gates. These are respectively called the gate of Life, of Death, of Riches, and of Poverty.

"In the centre (she said) was a tree, whose top was an arrow's flight from the ground, with leaves of emerald, and golden fruit. Of this tree she required a branch, and again renewed her assurance of the price which she would pay for the acquisition. Prasildo joyfully promised it, and would have promised sun, moon, and stars, as easily as the achievement of the adventure; upon which he immediately departs.

"The lady, it appears, dispatched him to the garden of Medusa[19], for so it was called, that he might find a cure for his love in absence and in travel : or, if he reached the spot, might find there a yet surer remedy for his distemper. For the sight of Medusa, who was to be found standing under the wonderful tree, occasioned every one to forget the errand he came on, and, if he had any speech with the dame, his very name and self.

"Prasildo, departing on this forlorn enterprise, traversed Egypt, and arriving near the mountains of Barca, encounters an old man, to whom he relates the object of his expedition.

"The old man assures him that fortune could not have directed him to a better counsellor, and immediately furnishes him with his instructions.

---

[19] Designed, I suppose, as the type of conscience; as one "whose sight would make him forget the errand on which he came," &c.

"He begins by telling him that the gates of Life and of Death are never used as entrances to the enchanted enclosure; and that it is only through the gate of Poverty that man can penetrate into the garden of Medusa. He next informs him that Medusa herself guards the marvellous tree; whose appearance deprives whoever sets eyes on her of his memory; but that she is to be terrified into flight by the reflection of her own face.

"He therefore counsels Prasildo to provide himself with a shield of looking-glass, being in other respects naked; for such appearance is a fitting guise for entering the gate of Poverty. This (he observes) is the most terrible and the most severely guarded of all, being watched by Misery and Shame, Cold, Hunger, Melancholy, and Scorn. "There," said he, "is to be seen Roguery stretched upon the ground, and covered with itch, and (in strange union,) Industry and Laziness, Compassion and Desperation.

"Having succeeded in the enterprise, and torn off a branch of the tree, you will seek the opposite gate," he pursues, " by which you are to retreat; and will there find Wealth seated, and on the watch. Here you are to make an offering of a portion of the branch, that Avarice, who plays the porter, may open to you quickly; a wretch who asks the more, the more you give. Here, too, you will see Pomp and Honour, Flattery and Hospitality, Ambition, Grandeur, and Favour : then Inquietude and Torment, Jealousy, Suspicion, Fear, Solicitude, and Terror. Behind the door stand Hate, and Envy with a bow for ever bent."

"Prasildo having received his full instructions, now crosses the desert, and, after thirty days' journey, arrives at the garden. Here he easily passes the gate of Poverty, the entry of which no one defends. On the contrary, there ever stands some one near it, to encourage and invite. "Having entered the inclosure, he advances, holding his shield of glass before his eyes; and reaching the tree, against which Medusa was leaning, the Fairy, who raises her head at his approach, and beholds herself in the mirror, takes to flight; scared, it seems, by seeing reflected in it the head of a serpent; though in other eyes her beauty is divine.[20] Prasildo, hearing the Fairy fly, uncovers his eyes, which were before protected by his shield, and leaving her to escape, goes directly to the tree, from which he severs a branch. Then, pursuing the directions received, makes for the opposite gate, where he sees Wealth, surrounded by her followers. This gate, which is of load-stone, never opens without noise, and is for the most part shut : Fatigue and Fraud are the guides who conduct to it. It is, however, sometimes open; but requires both luck and courage to enable any one to profit by the chance. It was open the day Prasildo came, and he made the offering of half the bough, as he was instructed, and escaped with the remainder of his prize.

[20] The circumstance of Medusa not being able to contemplate the reflection of her own hideous appearance, though beautiful in the sight of others; the fact of no one being able to win the golden bough which she kept, but by refraining from looking her in the face; and other circumstances, confirm the conjecture which I have hazarded in a preceding note.

"Transported with pleasure, he issues from the garden, passes through Nubia, crosses the Arabian Gulf with a fair wind, and journeys day and night till he arrives in Babylon.

"Arrived there, he sends immediate news of his success to Tisbina, who is in an agony at learning the unexpected result of her device. Iroldo is rendered equally miserable, but insists upon the necessity of her redeeming her promise, though he knows he cannot survive its execution. She feels that she can as ill survive Iroldo; and they at last resolve, that faith must be kept with Prasildo, and that they will both die. They accordingly send to an aged apothecary for a deadly draught, which they divide between them; and each having swallowed a due portion, Iroldo covers his face and throws himself on his bed, while the yet more miserable Tisbina proceeds to the residence of Prasildo. Here she attempts to dissemble her sorrow and to feign a cheerfulness, foreign to her heart. But Prasildo detects the imposture, and at last extorts a full confession of the truth. This declared, he reproaches her, as having little faith in his generosity, with a bursting heart renounces the proffered happiness, and dismisses her with an affectionate kiss.

"Tisbina, who had assured him that if she had known him first, she should have loved him as devotedly as she did her husband, now departs, overflowing with gratitude, and returns to Iroldo who was still unaffected by the draught, but prostrate on the bed. She relates to him the sacrifice of her lover. The husband springs from his couch, thanks God for this last mercy, and invokes every blessing upon the head of Prasildo. While he is yet praying, he sees the countenance of Tisbina change, who sinks, as if overcome by sleep. The husband sees the operation of the drink with horror, and is transported from his short fit of pleasure, to a state of the most agonizing despair.

"The situation of Prasildo is scarcely less intolerable; who locked himself up in his chamber, in order to indulge his grief in solitude, upon the departure of Tisbina. While he is shut up in darkness, the ancient apothecary calls, and tells his valet that Prasildo's life depends upon his immediate admission to him. The valet was a native of Casazzo, of a merry humour and full of faith and attachment, diligent, active, and experienced in all his duties; but of a frankness which sometimes gave his master offence. This man, having a master-key, admits the apothecary; who excusing the intrusion by his zeal for Prasildo's repose, informs him that he had that morning furnished the chambermaid of Tisbina with a potion, by her mistress's order, which he believed was destined for his destruction, as Tisbina had been shortly afterwards traced to his house; but adds, that he need be under no apprehension, even if he has swallowed the draught: since, in the apprehension of mischief, he had substituted a mere sleeping-potion, the effects of which were only calculated to last for a few hours.

"Prasildo, transported with joy, immediately flies in search of Iroldo, whose stronger constitution had as yet resisted the soporific, and informs him of the joyful tidings of the apothecary. Iroldo receives the news in such a manner as might have been expected, and concludes with making Prasildo a return such as he had never looked for. In a transport of gratitude, he insists on his receiving Tisbina, and accordingly departs from Babylon, leaving her yet asleep. On waking, she is combated by opposing feelings;

but at length, as the generosity of Prasildo had made more impression on her heart, than she was willing to confess, even to herself, yields to Iroldo's will, and takes Prasildo for her husband."

The damsel was yet speaking, when a loud cry was heard, which filled her with consternation. Rinaldo however, re-assuring her as he best could, pressed forward through the wood (for they were then in the centre of one) towards the quarter from which it proceeded.

He soon perceived a giant standing under a vaulted cavern, with a large club in his hand, and of an appearance to have struck the boldest spirit with dread. On each side of the cavern was chained a griffin, who, together with the giant, were stationed there for the protection of the horse which was once Argalia's.

This monster of enchantment was the creature.
For of a mare, composed of spark and flame,
(Strange wonder, and beyond the laws of nature)
Made pregnant by the wind, the courser came;
Matchless in vigour, speed, and form and feature.
Such was his birth, and Rabican his name :
Who, with his fellow-steeds, disdain'd to share
The proffer'd corn or grass, and fed on air.

This marvellous horse being driven away by Ferrau, in the wood of Arden, previous to his fatal encounter with Argalia, who had possessed himself of him by enchantment, on finding himself at liberty, returned to his native cavern, and was here stabled under the protection of the giant and the griffins. Towards these Rinaldo advances with deliberate valour, over ground whitened with the bones of their victims. He is the first to smite at the giant, but his stroke is rendered of no effect by the enchanted helmet of his adversary. In a second blow he is more fortunate; but his adversary, though wounded near the heart, escapes, and looses his griffins. One of these immediately seizes the giant by a foot: rises with him into the sky, hovers over Rinaldo's head, and at length drops his burden, with intent to crush the intruder. Rinaldo, however, who was as remarkable for his activity, as for his strength and courage, shuns the descending mischief, and the giant falls to the ground crushed, without harm to the paladin. In the meantime, the other griffin, having towered in air, pounces upon Rinaldo, who, watching his opportunity, wounds her desperately in her descent. She has, however, strength enough to soar a second flight, and swooping upon Rinaldo's helmet, loosens its circle with her claws; tear it she could not, since this was the enchanted helmet, which was once the head-piece of Mambrino.

In this manner the griffin repeats her attacks, and Rinaldo fends and parries as he can; while the damsel stands trembling near, and witnesses the contest.

The battle still continued, rendered more terrible by the approach of night; when Rinaldo, fearing he should not be able to distinguish his enemy, determined upon a desperate expedient, in order to bring it to a conclusion. He fell, as if fainting from his wounds, and on the close approach of the griffin, dealt her a blow, which sheared away one of her wings. The beast, though sinking, griped him fast with her talons, digging through plate and mail : but Rinaldo plied his sword in utter desperation, and at last accomplished her destruction.

The damsel now entreats Rinaldo to mount and proceed; but he thinks the adventure ill accomplished, and proceeds towards the entrance of the cavern. This was secured by a door,

Whose marble pannel a mosaic fill'd
Of pearl and emerald, sown with care so nice;
That he who saw the piece, if little skill'd,
Might deem it was a treasure passing price.
In the mid-picture lay a damsel kill'd;
And, writ in golden letters, the device
This legend bore : " Let whoso passes, plight
His word to 'venge my death, and do me right;
"Or he shall die the death; but if he swear
To slay the traitor who my death design'd;
The enchanted courser shall the warrior bear,
A courser that is swifter than the wind."

The prince stopt not to think; but plighted there
In solemn form, his promise, as enjoin'd;
His promise to avenge, alive or dead,
The slaughter'd damsel's blood, unjustly shed.
Then enters, and beholds the courser tied
With chains of gold, so famous for his speed.
With foot-cloth of white silk he was supplied,
And all things else convenient for his need.
Tho' coal-black all the rest, the tail was pied,
And starred with white the forehead of the steed;
And white one foot behind. Bayardo's might
Was more : but this had pass'd a dart in flight.

Rinaldo is delighted with his adventure, and, while surveying the steed, beholds a book, secured by a chain, in which was written in blood the history of the damsel's death.

The book related that Truffaldino, king of Baldacca, had a count for his neighbour, distinguished for his virtues and accomplishments, whom that evil-minded prince misliked on that very account. His name was Orisello, and Montefalcon was that of the castle where he resided. This lord had a sister as distinguished for her merit, called Albarosa, who loved Polindo, a noble knight of equal virtue and daring.

The castle was built upon a rock, and so well fortified, that Truffaldino, who had warred upon the count, though he had made several assaults upon it, had always been defeated in his attempts.

Things being in this state, Polindo, who had a great love for travel, and often wandered from court to court, arrived at that of Truffaldino; who, for his own evil views, shewed him great favour, and having acquired his confidence, promised him assistance in his designs upon Albarosa. As a means of forwarding these, he presents him with a castle of pleasure, situated a day's journey from Montefalcon; and Polindo having persuaded Albarosa to elope with him, carries her thither; but while they are supping together, with infinite delight, Truffaldino, who had entered the castle by a subterraneous passage, unknown to its new possessor, breaks in upon them with a party of his retainers, and binds them both. He then dictates a letter to the lady, which he orders her to send to her brother Orisello, in order to decoy him into his hands. She refuses; when the tyrant puts her to the torture, in the presence of Polindo, before whose eyes she expires, refusing compliance with her latest breath.

Rinaldo, having read this dreadful history, swears anew to avenge the treason, and, mounted upon Rabican, issues forth from the cavern. He and the damsel, however, have not ridden far, when the light fails them in a forest, where they dismount, secure their horses, and compose themselves to rest.

Beside the maid with zest Rinaldo sleeps;
For him, nor time, nor place, nor beauty move.
From whence we learn the antidote, which keeps
The heart and mind from that which is above
All other cure; that he, who sows and reaps,
Or tilts and tourneys, never dies of love :
But in this book I am ill read, nor can
Bolt, as I would, such matters to the bran.
And now the air on every side grew light,
Though the sun shew'd not yet his golden ray;
With few and fading stars the sky was dight,
And the glad birds rang out their matin lay.
Such was the season, neither day nor night;
When the maid view'd Rinaldo where he lay;
Who from her grassy couch before had crept,
And watch'd the weary warrior as he slept.
Of lively visage, though composed to rest,
The lusty knight in early youth appear'd,
Light in the flanks, and large across the chest;
And on his lip scarce bloom'd the manly beard.
On him the damsel gazed with alter'd breast,
To her by new-discovered gifts endear'd :
For slumber ever gives the sleeper's face
I know not what of loveliness and grace.

While the damsel is engaged in contemplating the knight, she is startled by a loud roar, and turning, sees a centaur with a live lion, which he had just taken, in one hand, and a club and three darts in the other. Rinaldo is at the same time awakened by the sound, and grasping his shield, or rather the remnant of it, which had been left by the griffin, advances to her assistance.

The centaur now leaves his prey, and flying to a little distance, launches his darts at the paladin. These he avoids by his agility, when the monster returns and charges him with his club. Rinaldo, thus pressed, shelters himself, by placing his back against a pine, and maintains the combat with Fusberta. The centaur, who had at first seemed to have the advantage, in being able to curvet about the knight, and threaten him behind and before, finding himself deprived of this double means of annoyance, leaves him, and gallops after the damsel, who had in the meantime seated herself upon her palfrey. From this he snatches her in fury, throws her on his own croup, and flies with her through the forest.

Rinaldo, who is this while engaged in mounting Rabican, follows; and, such is the swiftness of his horse, is almost immediately up with the beast; who, being overtaken on the brink of a rapid river, casts his burden into the stream, which carries it away. Rinaldo and the centaur again join in battle; at first on the shore, and afterwards in the water. The paladin at length slays his savage opponent : but having slain the monster, is in doubt what course to pursue.

He at last determines to proceed in the adventure in which he had embarked, being especially moved thereto, by the hope of delivering Orlando. Deprived then of the guidance of the poor damsel, he resolves to steer the same northern course in which she had before directed him.

Here, however, according to the author, Turpin leaves the story to return to Albraccn. Agrican was left there, surrounded and alone, in the midst of his enemies. Whilst he is thus reduced to the last extremities, he is saved by the very circumstance which threatened him with destruction. The soldiers of Angelica, closing upon him from all parts, had deserted their defences, and his own besieging army enter these pell mell, in a part where the wall is accessible.

In this way was Agrican rescued, the city taken by storm, and the miserable inhabitants put to the sword. Angelica, however, with some of the kings who were her defenders, and amongst whom was Truffaldino, saved herself in the citadel, which was planted upon a rock. Hither also came Sacripant when all beside was lost.

But though the situation of the fortress rendered it impregnable, it was scantily victualled and ill provided with other necessaries besides food. Under these circumstances, Angelica announced to those blockaded with her in the citadel, her intention to go in quest of assistance; and, having plighted her promise to come back within a certain period, set out, with the enchanted ring upon her finger.

Mounted on her palfrey, the damsel passed through the enemies' camp at night, without having occasion to avail herself of the talisman, and by sunrise was many miles clear of their encampment.

She at length arrives near Orgagna in Circassia, and here encounters an old man weeping bitterly, who entreats her assistance on behalf of his only son, who is dying of a fever. The damsel, who was well skilled in medicine, promises succour, turns her palfrey, and accompanies the elder.

This old man was a traitor, and his story a fiction, formed for the purpose of getting her into his hands. He was, it seems, employed to inveigle and capture damsels for the king of Orgagna, and for this purpose brought those who followed him to a tower, built over a river, which served him as a dungeon for his prisoners. Angelica following him thither, the door closed upon her, and she found herself a captive with many other dames and damsels. Amongst these was Flordelis, the lady of Brandimart, who, when cast into the river by the centaur, had drifted with the current, and was taken up more dead than alive, by the wicked elder. She now relates her adventures to Angelica, and tells her how she was going, accompanied by Rinaldo, to the garden of Dragontina, where Orlando, Brandimart, and many other valiant knights were enchanted by that fairy.

Angelica treasures up their history in her mind, as useful to the purpose which she had in hand, and on the door of the tower opening, to admit a new victim, slips the ring into her mouth and escapes.

Being again at liberty, she sets out for the garden of Dragontina, and, entering it unseen, disenchants Orlando, Brandimart, and the rest, by a touch of her talisman. These she conjures to assist her in the recovery of her kingdom, and all depart together for Albracca.

In the meantime a revolution had taken place in the citadel of that metropolis. Truffaldino, always false, had surprised Sacripant, and the other wounded princes in their beds, and cast them into prison. This done, he sent a messenger to Agrican, with an offer to deliver the fortress into his hands. Agrican, however, received the proposal in a manner little expected by Truffaldino, whom he reviled as a traitor and a coward; declared that he would never be indebted to fraud, for that which he could have by force; said he knew the extremities of the garrison, which must soon be his, and declared, that as soon as the place was in his possession, he would hang up Truffaldino by the heels.

Soon after this, Orlando, with his friendly squadron of knights (nine in number), with Angelica in the midst of them, arrives before Albracca; and charging through the camp of Agrican, arrives at the foot of the citadel : this is, however, kept against them by Truffaldino, who appears upon the walls, and declares that he will only admit Orlando and his followers, on their swearing to protect him for ever from the vengeance of Sacripant and the others; whom, for his own safety, he has been under the necessity of casting into prison. Orlando indignantly refuses; but, conjured by Angelica, consents; as do the others who accompany him; and after the oath has been taken as enjoined, the squadron enters the fortress.

This, however, is found so destitute of food, that a sally is resolved upon for the purpose of provisioning it : it is to be made by Orlando, Brandimart, Adrian, Clarion, and Uberto of the Lion; while Gryphon and Aquilant remain at home for the protection of Angelica and the citadel.

Orlando and his friends having made the warder lower his drawbridge, ride boldly towards the enemy's camp; and Agrican, marking their scanty number, bids his squadrons stand apart, and leave a fair field for himself and Orlando, who engage in a desperate duel. While they are employed in this, with little vantage on either side, and to their mutual astonishment at finding themselves so equally matched, a loud larum is heard from the citadel, which announces the arrival of succours.

This was an army, raised by Galaphron, for the relief of Albracca; the vanguard commanded by a vassal giant; the second body by Marphisa, a young Indian queen, who had made a vow in her infancy, never to lay aside her armour, till she had taken three kings prisoners, to wit, Charlemagne, Gradasso, and Agrican; while the rear-guard was conducted by Galaphron himself. The van-guard, led by the giant, is immediately engaged with the besiegers; and its leader, armed with an immense hammer, deals such destruction amongst their ranks, that all is speedily in confusion and disarray.

Agrican, witnessing the rout of his followers, now entreats Orlando, for his lady's love, that their combat may be suspended till the morrow, in order to give him an opportunity of rallying the fugitives. This Orlando not only grants, but offers to assist him in his design. The offer is, however, courteously declined by Agrican, who, flying in pursuit of the giant, unhorses him, and leaves him desperately wounded to the daggers of his followers. He himself charges the troops who come under the giant's conduct; and the tide of battle is turned.

No attempt to stop the confusion of the vanguard is made by Marphisa, who this time was retired from the field, and sleeping under a tree.

But first the queen her chamber-wench bespoke.

"Attend to my command," Marphisa said,
And when thou seest our Indian army broke,
And Galaphron, its royal leader, dead,
When all these things shall be, 'twere time I woke,
Then, bring my steed and rouse me from my bed.
But till these things shall be, such care delay,
"'Tis then this single arm shall change the day."

Galaphron now observing the rout of his vanguard, determines to retrieve things, or perish in the attempt. With this resolution he spurs towards the enemy; when Angelica, beholding his danger from the walls, sends a messenger to Orlando, to entreat his assistance for her father; reminding him that he fought beneath her eyes.

The author here leaves the story suspended, and returns to Rinaldo; who journeying. northward, in the direction which Flordelis, the damsel of Brandimart, had first given him, arrives at a fountain; where he finds a cavalier weeping upon the ground. Having long observed his grief in silence, he at length dismounts from his horse, and entreats the sorrowing knight to inform him of its cause.

The stranger tells him that his misery is such as can find no remedy but in death : nor does the fear of that oppress him ; but the knowledge that his death must be followed by that of another, llinaldo entreats him to explain how this can be, and prevails on him to relate his history at length.

This the stranger began in the following manner : " About twenty days' journey from hence is situated the famous city of Babylon, of which Tisbina was the wonder; a lady alike renowned for her charms and virtues. Of this treasure I became the possessor; yet, having possessed her, found it my cruel duty to vield her to another. For two vears afterwards I wandered, almost deprived of my reason; but time at last brought with it some alleviation of my sorrow. To this common remedy of grief was united the reflection that I had resigned her to the most virtuous and most courteous of men; and that, however dear it might cost me, it was impossible to repent my sacrifice.

"While I was thus wandering, my evil fortune led me into Orgagna, whose rightful king, Poliphernus, was absent with the army of Agrican; his kingdom having, during his absence, fallen into the possession of an evil woman, who makes all strangers her prey. This enchantress (for such she is), whose name is Falerina, has a beautiful garden, which is only open towards the east; where a serpent keeps the gate, to whom Falerina gives her unfortunate prisoners to be devoured. The names of these are paired, a cavalier and a lady, according to the order of their arrival; and a couple is thus every day offered to the monster.

"I was amongst the prisoners of Falerina; when tidings of my imprisonment, for my greater misfortune, reached the ears of Prasildo, the noble gentleman to whom I had relinquished Tisbina. Unknown to me, he immediately set out for the enchanted garden, loaded with treasure, with which he attempted to accomplish my release. All his endeavours, however, were vain; and desperate of accomplishing it in any other way, he offered himself as a victim in my place. This offer was accepted : I was thrust out of the dungeon, and he remains a prisoner in my stead. This day is that appointed for his sacrifice, which shall not be consummated, whilst I am alive : for it is my resolution, when he is led out of prison to be conducted to the place of punishment, to attack his guards and perish in his defence. My single source of grief is, that I shall not be able to purchase his deliverance with my life."

Rinaldo bids the stranger be of better cheer, and offers to join him in the attack of Prasildo's guards, to which Iroldo, who conceives this will be a useless sacrifice of life, very unwillingly accedes.

The issue of the attempt is, however, very different from what Iroldo had anticipated. The rabble, who were conducting two prisoners to the place of execution, are set upon by the knights, and scattered on all sides; principally by the valour of Rinaldo.

In the male prisoner Iroldo recognizes Prasildo, as he had expected; and the damsel turns out to be Flordelis. Rinaldo is now impatient to crown his victory with the destruction of the enchanted garden; but the damsel, his former guide, after vainly seeking to terrify him by a description of the various monsters and enchantments by which it was guarded, reminds him of the imprisonment of Orlando, and his unaccomplished promise to achieve the destruction of the garden of Dragontina. This consideration prevails over his anxiety to demolish that of Falerina; and in company with his two friends and the damsel, who all become Christians in admiration of his prowess and in gratitude for their deliverance, proceeds on his journey towards the garden of Dragontina.

This however had been previously destroyed and effaced, even to the last vestige, by the talisman of Angelica.

The knights, pursuing their journey towards its former situation, meet on their way a fugitive from Agrican's army; who gives such an account of the prowess of a champion who fought upon the part of Angelica, that Rinaldo is persuaded this must have been Orlando; though all are at a loss to imagine how he could have been freed. They had not proceeded much farther, when they saw a warrior under some trees, to whom a damsel was presenting a horse. This warrior Flordelis recognized by her bearings for Marphisa, and who she especially counselled her companions to avoid. They, however, and more especially Rinaldo, treated the caution with contempt, and made boldly towards the virago.

As she is just mounting, to defy them to the joust, she is approached by an elderly man, all in tears, who relates the overthrow of Galaphron's vanguard, and entreats her assistance; which she promises to bestow, as soon as she shall have unhorsed and taken the approaching strangers.

Advancing against them, she first encounters and overthrows Iroldo and Prasildo in succession, who are made prisoners by some of Marphisa's followers, that were in waiting, together with the attendant damsel. She next meets Rinaldo, and breaks upon him an enormous lance, which had never yet failed her. Rinaldo too breaks his upon the damsel, and both, casting away their broken spears, encounter with their swords. Here Rinaldo's dextrous skill in defence, and the superior temper of Fusberta, give him a temporary advantage; and in parrying a blow of his opponent, he beats the faulchion out of her hand. Full of fury, the virago deals him a deadly blow on the face with her gauntletted hand in return, and makes him reel in his saddle; while Rabican wheels round and carries off his half-stupefied rider. Marphisa instantly springs to ground and regains her sword, and Rinaldo recovering himself again spurs his courser to the encounter.

In the mean time, Orlando, at the command of Angelica, had galloped to the assistance of Galaphron, at the head of his brave companions, and had again changed the fortune of the day. He and Agrican now meet a second time in the medley, and renew the contest with more fury than before; and Agrican, being at last convinced that it will be impossible for him to effect any thing against Albracca but by the destruction of Orlando, determines to bring the battle to a desperate issue, and in order to get his adversary into a place where they shall be secure from interruption, feigns to fly; and is followed by Orlando to an open space in a wood, in the middle of which is a fountain. Here, after mutual reproaches, they again charge each other with their swords, and still with doubtful success. Night closes upon the combatants, who have passed the greater part of the day in the interchange of blows.

The two champions again suspend their combat almost of necessity, and agree upon a truce till day-light. They accordingly lie down together and engage in a friendly conversation. During this Agrican makes out his antagonist to be Orlando; and Orlando seizes the opportunity to attempt his conversion. Agrican, however, receives the proposal with utter contempt, and observes that love and arms are the only subjects of conversation becoming a knight.

This change of theme almost necessarily leads to the mention of Angelica, and the rivals, being kindled by the discourse which ensues between them, into new animosity, remount their horses and attack each other in the dark.

The contest is thus continued with various success, and day breaks upon this desperate and unheard-of duel. At length, however, the fortune of Orlando prevails, and he after receiving many desperate contusions (for wounded he could not be), inflicts a deadly gash in his adversary's side.

Agrican is now deserted by his lofty spirit, and demands baptism from the hands of Orlando :

While tears descending bathed his manly face,
The gentle count dismounted to his aid,
Then locked the wounded knight in his embrace,
Upon the fountain's grassy border laid :
And kiss'd his fading lips, and sought his grace,
And of the mischief done forgiveness prayed.
The speechless Tartar king his head inclin'd,
And with the cross his brows Orlando sign'd.
When having to his sorrow found that he
Was breathless, and all vital warmth was fled;
He weened his gallant spirit was set free,
And by the crystal fountain left him dead;
Clad as he was in armour cap-a-pe,
With sword in hand, and crown upon his head :
Then first towards his courser turn'd his view,
And in that steed the good Bayardo knew.

He is assured of this by a closer examination of the gentle horse, who comes neighing to greet the kinsman and comrade of his master.

Mounted upon him, and leading his own Brigliadoro, the count leaves the place, but has not rode far, before he hears the clash of weapons; when, having first secured Brigliadoro, he rides in the direction of the sound; and, guided by it, discovers a damsel, whom three giants were conducting, with a camel and much treasure, which they had carried away by force. One of the giants had charge of the lady; while the other two maintained a combat with a cavalier : but this story is broken off, by the author, who hastens to tell the effects, produced by the death of Agrican.

All was rout and dismay in the Tartarian army; and Galaphron entering the enemy's camp, set free Astolpho and the other prisoners, who were detained there. Astolpho is scarcely presented to Angelica, before he demands the means of avenging himself on the enemy, and being furnished with a horse and arms, immediately returns into the field. Here he is fortunate enough to meet one clad in his own armour, and armed with the enchanted lance.

Of these he immediately repossesses himself, and joins Galaphron and his troops, who had pursued the flying enemy to the banks of a river, fast by where Rinaldo and Marphisa were still engaged. Marphisa was protected by enchanted harness, yet was armed with but half a sword; which, as related, was severed by Fusberta. On the other hand, the greater part of Rinaldo's defensive armour had been hewed away.

Galaphron instantly knows Marphisa by her cognizance, but is at a loss to distinguish Rinaldo; till, observing Rabican, who had belonged to Argalia, he conceived that he saw in him the murderer of his son. Under this persuasion he rode at Rinaldo, and smote him with all his force, when Marphisa, enraged at this interference, immediately turned her arms against her aged commander. Brandimart and others coming up, rescue him from the hands of the virago, whom they take for some warrior of the Tartar troops; when Rinaldo, as generous as Marphisa, not enduring to see his former enemy overlaid with odds, joins her against those with whom she is now engaged. The main body of Galaphron's army coming up, reinforces the enemies of Marphisa; who is on her part supported by the arrival of her own division, by whose succour, joined to that of Rinaldo, she is enabled to repel the assailants.

All this time, Iroldo, Prasildo, and Flordelis, were standing at some distance, and the damsel of Marphisa, was entertaining them with a history of the feats and prowess of her mistress. Flordelis is by this alarmed for the safety of Brandimart, one of the first who had assailed Marphisa, and goes in search of him amongst the warriors, whom the virago and Rinaldo had scattered, and who were making, in utter rout and confusion, for Albracca. She, however, to her infinite content, finds him safe and standing apart from the fray, he having separated from the enemies of Marphisa, after she was oppressed by numbers. The happy lovers, thus re-united, retire into a neighbouring wood, and after giving a loose to their mutual tenderness fall asleep upon the grass.

Here, however, a new and unexpected peril was impending. Their caresses were unfortunately overseen by a hermit, who dabbled in necromancy, and who, excited by the beauties of Flordelis, determined on making her his prize. Among other secrets, he was possessed of a root, which had the faculty of throwing the person to whom it was applied, provided it touched any part of the naked body, into a profound and indissoluble sleep. Armed with this, he approaches Flordelis, lifts her coats, and applies it to her thigh. Having thus so riveted her natural slumber, that he was sure she could not wake for an hour to come, the hermit snatches her up, and bears her off; being afraid to try the virtues of his root upon Brandimart, lest he should awake before the charm was consummated.

Brandimart slept soundly till he was awakened by a loud noise. At the same moment he missed Flordelis : yet, notwithstanding his unutterable grief, approached the quarter, from whence the sound proceeded, in which he distinguished the cries of a woman in distress.

On his arrival he found three giants, who were conducting a file of camels. Two of them followed, and another preceded the string, leading one, on which was seated a damsel, with dishevelled hair and weeping bitterly. In her Brandimart believed that he recognised Flordelis, and galloped in fury against the ravishers.

The giants instantly prepare to resist him, and in the combat which follows, he is put to great peril, and loses his horse.

It is at this moment that Orlando, who had lately slain Agrican, comes to his succour. His assistance renders the combat more equal : but Brandimart, though he has killed one of the giants, is beaten down by another. Orlando, however, avenges him on his enemy, and clears the field. He has now leisure to look to his bleeding friend, and finding there is yet life in him, consigns him to the care of the rescued damsel, who applies the proper medicaments to his wounds.

Marphisa and Rinaldo were this while still in full pursuit of their enemies, who found refuge within the citadel of Albracca. Marphisa having chased them up to the gates, menaced Galaphron with vengeance; and, indeed, she and Rinaldo had now a common cause. Marphisa on account of her recent quarrel with her former leader; and Rinaldo since the fountain of hate had disposed him to enmity with Angelica, and the oath, he had sworn on winning Rabican, bound him to take vengeance on Truffaldino, one of her defenders. They accordingly sit down before the place, and, on the second day, Rinaldo appears beneath the walls, sounds his horn and defies Truffaldino, king of Baldacca by the titles of traitor, renegado and tyrant.

There were at. this time, within the fortress, many warriors who had sworn to defend him against Sacripant and Torindo, whom he had imprisoned, and against all others whatsoever. Truffaldino calls on these to fulfil their engagement, and several knights, with the traitor king in the midst of them, descend from the citadel to do battle with Rinaldo, on his behalf.

These were the brothers Gryphon and Aquilant, who had enchanted horse and armour; Uberto, Adrian, and Clarion. They attack Rinaldo singly and successively. He soon defeats the two first comers, but he finds himself better matched with Gryphon of the enchanted arms; with whom he engages in a long and doubtful battle, after a fruitless expostulation and attempt to negotiate on the part of Gryphon.

Leaving these, the author returns to Brandimart; who, restored to life by the skill of the damsel, whom he and Orlando rescued from the giants, is rendered desperate by the discovery, that she is not Flordelis. He curses the hour in which he was rescued from death, as well as that in which he was born, and recapitulates all the circumstances of his life in the following apostrophe :

"Thou took'st me, Fortune, from a royal dome,
(Such early blow thy deadly malice gave;)
And I, thus ravished from my noble home,
In other lands was sold to be a slave;
And now, long doomed in foreign climes to roam,
But her remember to whose breasts I clave;
(My father's and my country's name effaced,)
My mother's in my mind is only traced.
"Never did evil destiny so lour,
As upon me; to early bondage sold,
With one, entitled Lord o' the Sylvan Tower :
When, but to make me suffer sevenfold,
Softened awhile appear'd the faithless Power;
And the good Master of the Sylvan hold
Freed me; and having none his name to bear,
Of his broad lands and living made me heir.
"But Fortune had so marked me for her prey,
That to fill up the bitter cup of woe,
Fairest among the fair, a damsel gay
She chose in her displeasure to bestow;
Simply to take the precious prize away.
Then can I choose but sink beneath the blow ?
O thou, that hast renewed my fleeting breath,
Undo thy work, and give me back to death."

Orlando, and the charitable damsel sympathise deeply in his grief; and the lady, to prove, at least, that he was not single in his sorrows, begins the narration of her own adventures.

She informs him, that she was daughter and heir of the king of the Distant Isles, where all the treasure of the earth is accumulated. Gifted with beauty and destined to inherit such riches, two lovers came to demand her in marriage on the same day, Ordauro and Folderico; the one handsome and the other more than seventy years old. The first distinguished by his prowess, the second by his wisdom and riches. The damsel's

84

father inclined hi favour of Folderico; but the damsel hoped by a sleight to transfer herself to Ordauro.

She had accordingly obtained a boon from the monarch; and this was, that no one should have her to wife, who had not previously vanquished her in the foot-race. By this, she considered herself as secure of success; but Folderico countermined her stratagem. Being paired with her in the course, he had recourse to the expedient of dropping three golden apples, and the damsel was distanced by the same means as Atalanta. Thus the old man won his wife; who, however, determined on taking such vengeance as was in her power.

Here the lady, who was her own historian, observed Brandimart's distraction; who being charged with it, confessed that he had neither eyes nor ears but for Flordelis, and that he should never regain possession of himself, till she was found. On this the damsel and Orlando, who was mounted on Bayardo, and had resigned his Brigliadoro to Brandimart, as before related, offer to accompany him in an attempt to recover her, and they immediately proceed upon their search.

Flordelis, in the interval, had been carried off by the hermit to a cave; where she woke at the moment that a lion, who harboured there, sprang forth to punish the intrusion of the ravisher : who instantly dropt his plunder and fled. The beast, however, passing-by the proffered prey, follows and tears in pieces the hermit who had cast it down. Flordelis, while he is thus employed, escapes.

She, however, only gains a present respite from misfortune; for, flying at random, she falls into the hands of a hairy savage in the forest, who binds her to a tree with twigs; and then, gazing stupidly upon her, casts himself down at a little distance.

Brandimart was this while in pursuit of her, in the same wood, accompanied by Orlando and the damsel of the golden apples, who was seated upon his courser's croup. Orlando now entreats that she will finish her story, which she continues.

Folderico who had won the damsel, carried her to a tower, which he possessed upon the sea-shore, called Altamura, where he kept her, together with his treasure, under lock and key, and utterly secluded from the sight of man.[20]

But what will not love ? Ordauro who was also rich, though not so wealthy as Folderico, purchased a sumptuous palace in the immediate neighbourhood of Altamura, and at an immense cost made a subterraneous passage from his palace to the damsel's prison; by which he visited and enjoyed her without danger. At last, however, the lovers, tired of the restraint under which they carried on their intercourse, and emboldened by success, determined to make a desperate effort to escape.

With this view Ordauro communicates to Folderico news of his approaching nuptials with another daughter of Monodontes; for so was called the king of the Distant Isles; and invites him, as his brother-in-law, to the marriage feast. Folderico having carefully secured the gates of his tower, goes thither, and finding his wife installed as bride, becomes ferocious at the sight. Ordauro, however, with great difficulty, succeeds in appeasing him, by the assurance that she was a twin-sister of his own wife, to whom she bore a perfect resemblance; and, by bidding him return to his tower and satisfy himself of the fact. The means of proof appeared decisive, and accordingly Folderico accepts them. He finds his locks as they were left, and his wife, (who had returned by the subterraneous passage and changed her dress,) alone and overcome with melancholy. He again takes the way, which was somewhat circuitous, to the palace of Ordauro, and again finds her there, shining in all the festivity of a bride. He can no longer resist the conviction that the two persons, whom he had seen, were different women; lays aside his distrust, and even offers to convoy the bridegroom and his bride on a part of their journey towards Ordauro's natural home, to which he was returning.

A certain advantage was thus gained; since Folderico never left his tower, though locked, for above an hour, and

---

[20] As the author is indebted to Greek fable for the beginning, so he is to Norman story for this subsequent adventure, which is taken, with some variation, from an old fabliau. See Barbasan's or Le Grand's fabliaux. The story would seem to be of Eastern origin.

consequently would have soon discovered his loss, if the lovers had eloped in secret.

The party set out together; and at the end of the first day's journey, Folderico turns back and gallops to his tower. He is now first assured of his disgrace. Full of rage, he pursues his rival; but does not dare make any attempt to recover his wife, till he has separated Ordauro from his adherents. Having effected this by a stratagem, he attacks his retainers, and repossesses himself of the lady. He is destined to a short possession of the prize; for he is, on his retui-n, beset by giants, who seize her, and all his treasure; which the wife was carrying off as a dowry to her new lord. He himself escapes.

Orlando listened with curiosity to this relation : but Brandimart, who only thought upon Flordelis, separated from his companions in order to pursue a separate search. Whilst he is engaged in this, he hears her cries, and, directed by them, finds her bound to the tree. He dismounts from his horse to assist her, and is about to loosen her bonds, when he is attacked by the savage, armed with a rustic club and shield. This strange woodman is described as gifted with extraordinary strength of body, and distinguished by some strange propensities :

He dwelt in woods, and on their produce fed,
And drank the limpid brook which bubbled by :
And (such his nature) ever, it is said,
Wept, when he saw a clear and cloudless sky :
Since, fearful of the sign, he lived in dread,
That tempest, clouds, and cold, and rain were nigh,
But joy'd in thunder and in hail; since he
Hoped warmer suns and happier days to see.

This savage, but for the exclamation of Flordelis, would have surprised Brandimart in the act of untying her. Being warned by her of his danger, he guarded himself against his attacks, which required all his skill and courage to repel. He indeed hewed in pieces the rustic weapon with which he was armed; but the monster, closing with him, grasped him in his arms, and attempted to cast him down a precipice, when he fortunately escaped from his embrace. The savage finding himself foiled in this hope, and weaponless, now flew to a sapling, which he was trying to pluck up by its roots, when the knight killed him while engaged in the attempt. Brandimart now releases Flordelis, seats her on his horse's croup, and goes in pursuit of Orlando, from whom he had separated.

Whilst he is thus engaged, the author resumes the story of Albracca. Rinaldo was left in close combat with Gryphon, whom he at last stunned with a desperate blow. When Aquilant, believing his brother killed, took up the conqueror. Gryphon, however, reviving from the effects of the stroke, returned to the charge.

Marphisa seeing Rinaldo thus oppressed with odds, came to his assistance; and others again of those sworn to defend Truffaldino, who was an unwilling spectator of the fray, took part against her and Rinaldo. Orlando was, this while, pursuing his way in search of Brandimart, while Brandimart as vainly sought him through the forest.

Whilst Orlando is thus engaged, he sees a damsel issue from a wood upon a palfrey, who bears a book and horn. Addressing herself to the count, she tells him, that, if he is what his countenance bespeaks him, the fairest adventure awaits him, which ever was achieved by knight; and which, indeed, had hitherto foiled the prowess of all who had attempted it, who remained prisoners in the enchanted garden, which she invites him (if he has the courage sufficient for such an adventure) to attack. Orlando accepts the proposal with rapture; the damsel presents him with the book and horn; both necessary for the achievement of the enterprize; and, having instructed him in the use of them, retires to a distance.

Orlando accordingly, having first disposed of the other damsel whom he carried behind him, sounds the bugle, and a rock opens, from which issue two ferocious bulls, with horns of iron, and strangely coloured hair turned contrary to the natural grain :

And sometimes green; now black, now white it seemed,
Now yellow, and now red; and ever gleamed.

Orlando learned from the book, by whose rules he was to proceed, that he was to bind these beasts; and this done, was to enter the opening, from which they sallied, and plow with them the space within. Such was to be his first labour.

The bulls long maintained a severe fight with the champion, and often tossed, though they could not gore him : at length he so fatigued them by repeated blows from Durindana, (for their skin was as impenetrable as his own,) that he was enabled to master them, seized them by their horns, and bound them separately, with Bayardo's bridle, to an adjoining column, which was the monument of the king Bavardo. He then made a plow of Durindana, the point of which served as a share and the hilt as a handle, yoked the bulls to the instrument, and having torn off the limb of a tree for a whip, ploughed the field, as he was directed. The work accomplished, he loosed his beasts, who ran roaring through the wood, and disappeared behind a mountain.

Orlando now devoutly thanks God for his first success, and the damsel of the book and horn, having dismounted from the palfrey in the meadow, wreaths her brows with the flowers which it produced. Orlando, however, does not allow himself a longer truce, but sounds a second challenge on his enchanted bugle.

Upon the second sound, the earth trembles, and a neighbouring hill vomits forth flame; which is followed by the appearance of a fiery dragon. The damsel of the golden apples is now about to fly; but she of the book and horn bids her

"in faith and hope, stand near,

For only he who proves the quest need fear."

The damsel of the golden apples, who resented Orlando's coldness during their journey through the forest, observes she is glad that he only is in danger, and that she cannot regret what may happen to him;

"In that there lives not a more worthless wight." This reproach reaches Orlando's ears, as he consults his book. This guide taught him that his only means of safety consisted in cutting off the dragon's head, before he was consumed by the flame and venom, which issued from her mouth. The head cut off, he was to perform the labour of Jason, and sow the field in which he had laboured with the serpent's teeth. From these was to spring a crop of armed men; and, if he saved himself from their swords, he might esteem himself the flower of chivalry.

He has scarce learned his lesson, when the serpent is upon him. Orlando protected himself from her assault with his shield; but this and all his armour was consumed by the flame which she vomited forth. He contends long with the monster, enveloped in fire and smoke, but at last separates her head at a blow. He immediately draws the teeth, puts them into his helmet, and sows them as the book had enjoined. The effect followed which had been foretold.

> First, feathers sprouting from the ground appear,
> By little and by little; then a crest;
> And next is seen the bust of cavalier,
> Furnish'd with manly limbs, and spreading chest.
> Foot in the front, and horsemen in the rear;
> They rise and shout, and lay the lance in rest;
> And, drums and trumpets sounding to the charge,
> Level the spear, and lift the covering targe.

Orlando, however, though he had neither lance nor shield left him, soon reaps this harvest with Durindana; and the seed of the serpent thus springs and perishes in a day.

The victory achieved, he blows the third and last blast upon his horn, which the author thus prefaces :

> These dragons and these gardens, made by spell,
> And dog, and book by witch or wizard writ,
> And savage hairy man, and giant fell,
> And human face, to monstrous form ill fit,
> Are food for ignorance, which you may well
> Decypher, that are blest with shrewder wit :
> Then muse upon the doctrine sage and sound,
> Which lies conceal'd beneath this rugged ground.[21]
> Such matter as is excellent and rare,
> And things of scent or savour, rich or fine,

---

[21] The Italian reader will here again trace some lines of Dante.

In open hand we do not loosely bear;
Nor cast such pearls to be defiled of swine.
Nature, great mistress, teaches better care,
Who loves the flower with fencing thorns to twine;
And covers well her fruits, and things of mark;
The kernel with its stone, the tree with bark;
A safe defence from bird, and beast, and storm;
And has conceal'd the yellow gold i' the ground,
Jewels, and what is rare for tint or form;
That these may be with cost and labour found.
And vain and witless is th' unwary swarm
Who show their wealth, if they with wealth abound,
The mark, at which knave, thief, and cheater level;
And so by matchless folly tempt the devil.
As duly would it seem to square with reason,
That good should be with toil and trouble bought.
And to obtain it otherwise were treason,
Than by activity of deed and thought.
'Tis thus we see, that art and labour season
The victual, which without their aid is nought;
And simple viands, in their nature good,
Convert to sweeter, and more savoury food.
If Homer's Odyssey appear compounded
Of lying legends, deem not these unfit;
Nor, reading of some god or goddess wounded,
Let this aught scandalize your weaker wit :
For who the secrets of the sage has sounded,
Well knows, that for the sage, the poet writ;
And veils a different thing, from that which lies
Open to them, who see but with their eyes.
But stop not ye, content, at the outer rind;
Be not as these, but seek what is within;
For if no better nourishment you find,
You will have made small progress for your sin ,
And see in these strange emblems ill-divined,
But sick men's dreams, and fables. Then begin

A better task, their secret meaning measure,
And turn the stubborn soil for hidden treasure.

Returning to the story, Orlando sounded his horn a third time; and, on the echo dying away, was disappointed by the appearance of a little white bitch-hound.

This, the damsel of the book, in hopes to stay the count, who was now disposed to depart, assured him was that which was to crown his toils.

She explains herself, by informing him, that in a neighbouring lake is an island, the residence of the Fata, Morgana, whom God has set over riches; which she

"Distributes in the bowels of the mount,
Whence they are dug with long fatigue and pain;
And hides them in the river and the fount,
In India; where ants work the golden vein.
Nor let the tale seem strange, which I recount,
Since two fair fishes feed upon the grain.
Now good Morgana the bitch-hound has sent
To guerdon thee with treasure and content :
"The wondrous Fay, for various riches vaunted,
Mistress of all that seas or earth enfold,
Is owner of a hind, in this enchanted;
That she is white, and armed with horns of gold;
And that by her no forest long is haunted,
Still restless and impatient of a hold.
Her many hunters vainly seek to catch;
But you may take her with this little brach.
"Who soon shall rouse her from her secret lair,
Yelping upon the trail with questing cry :
Thou shalt pursue, thro' holt or desert bare,
Though hound and hart more swift than arrow fly:
Six days shalt thou pursue the flying pair;
But on the seventh cease the chase to ply.
Since in a fount the milk-white hind shall soil,[22]

_____

[22] The technical phrase for a stag taking the water : as he usually does when distressed. Hence our view-hollo of "Tayo!" for the stag, is taken from the old

And thou be guerdon'd for thy tedious toil.
"Six times a-day (such riches shalt thou measure)
She sheds her horns; which yield an hundred weight.
And thus shalt thou collect such mighty treasure
As may defy the wit of man to rate;
Thrice blest, if countless wealth can purchase pleasure;
To this perchance deserve a happier fate;
And with the hind obtain what is above
That precious prize, the beauteous fairy's love."

Orlando however treats the temptation with contempt, and unwillingly seating the damsel of the golden apples behind him, casts down the book and horn, and departs.

Proceeding with her, he arrives at a bridge, where he meets with an armed cavalier, who claims the damsel as his own. This turns out to be Ordauro, to whom Orlando resigns her with great satisfaction, and pursues his journey to Albracca.

Here the strife was still continued between Rinaldo and Marphisa, united on the one part; and Gryphon and Aquilant, and all those confederated to defend Truffaldino, on the other. Rinaldo having in this gained some advantage over his immediate opponents, Truffaldino, who was present, fled into the citadel. This put a short stop to hostilities, and the combat was suspended till the ensuing day; when Truffaldino was to be again produced, and to abide its issue.

In this interval two important circumstances occur. Astolpho (who was Agrican's prisoner, when those, who entered Albracca with Angelica, took the engagement to defend Truffaldino) learning from Gryphon, that Rinaldo had been his antagonist, changes sides, and goes over to his cousin.

French cry of "Taihors," or "out of the swamp!" as our "Tally ho !" for the fox, is derived from "Taillis hors!" or "out of cover !" which last etymology we learn from Lady Juliana Berners. All our hunting phraseology indeed is Norman; even where we should be least inclined to trace it to such a source. Thus the cry of "Hiloicks! Hiloicks!" used by us in trying a cover, we find in her precepts to be "Illocques, Illocques!" or "There! There!" The Normans indeed formed both our hunting code and hunting vocabulary. See many well founded allusions to this in Ivanhoe.

To counterbalance this loss to the besieged, Orlando arrives in Albracca, and is received with open arms by Angelica.

On the ensuing day the combat is renewed between the former parties with the addition of Astolpho on one side, and of Orlando on the other. In this Orlando and Rinaldo single each other out, and after bitter reproaches, Rinaldo reproving Orlando for his defence of a traitour, and Orlando twitting Rinaldo for his robberies and evil life, engage in a furious combat; but here Orlando is ill seconded by Bayardo, who will not advance against his own master.

At this moment Rinaldo sees Truffaldino treacherously unhorse Astolpho, and pursuing him, (for the traitour flies upon his approach,) comes up with him before he is overtaken by his defenders, makes him prisoner, and ties him by the feet to Rabican's tail. With the wretch thus suspended, he gallops off at full speed; the superior swiftness of Rabican rendering all interference on the behalf of Truffaldino impossible; and drags him at his horse's heels till he is dashed in pieces.

Whilst he is running this cruel course, Rinaldo thunders out reproaches and threats against the abettors of the tyrant; and Orlando, who had now obtained his own horse, Brigliadoro, through the arrival of Brandimart, who joins him, renews his battle with Rinaldo on personal grounds, the others considering themselves released from the necessity of fighting him by the death of Truffaldino.

Night however separates the two combatants, Rinaldo returning to Marphisa's camp, and Orlando to the citadel of Albracca.

Here Orlando is received with all love and honour by Angelica; who is, however, sighing in her heart for Rinaldo, and, with this view, declares she will attend the duel which was to be renewed on the morrow, and sends Sacripant, delighted with the task, to demand a safeconduct for her from Marphisa. Previously however to Orlando's taking the field, she demands of him a boon; swearing she will make him lord of her person, if he will promise to undertake an adventure upon her bidding; and avails herself of this promise, the next day, when the strife is at its hottest; telling Orlando that enough has been done for honour, and entreating him now to depart upon the promised quest; which was no other than the destruction of Falerina's garden hi the kingdom of Orgagna.

The combatants being separated, and Orlando departed, Angelica seeks to communicate with Rinaldo, but in vain; and returns disconsolate to Albracca, from whence she sends a damsel to Rinaldo with Bayardo, whom Orlando had dispatched to that fortress on receiving Brigliadoro from Brand imart; but Rinaldo remains unmoved by these various acts of kindness.

The scene is now again changed, and Orlando, whom Angelica had dispatched upon what she conceived a fatal enterprise, pursues his way towards Orgagna.

He arrives at a bridge, on which is seen a cavalier, armed at all points, and mounted, as if for its defence. Near this was seen a beautiful damsel, suspended by her hair to a pine, and weeping bitterly. Orlando immediately moves to her relief; but is exhorted by the armed cavalier to leave her to a fate, which she had well deserved by her wickedness. In proof of which he proceeds to relate her adventures.

"My name," pursued the knight, " is Uldano, and hers Origilla. We were both born in the city of Bactria, and I, from earliest infancy, conceived a passion for her, which grew with my growth, and derived strength even from her fickleness. Another youth, of the name of Lucrino, loved her equally with myself; and both were so well kept hi play by her artifices, that each believed himself to be favoured.

"Being at length impatient of longer delay, I threw myself at her feet, and entreated her to take compassion on my torments. She appeared to meet my passion half-way; but told me, there was but one mode in which I could gratify my desires without the sacrifice of her honour, and suggested the following stratagem as the means.

"'You know,' said the damsel, 'that my brother, Corbirio, though scarcely arrived at manhood, was slain by Oringo in combat, a man grown, and trained to arms. To avenge this treason, my father has offered a large reward to him who shall take the murderer, and would soon find one who would undertake to execute his revenge. You shall bear the cognizance of Oringo, shall suffer yourself to be taken, and thus procure admission into my father's house. Here you shall receive the reward of your constancy, and I will afterwards effect your deliverance.'

"I, senseless as I was, gave into the snare, and had scarce departed, in order to assume the device and arms she suggested, when the traitress called to her my rival, Lucrino, and told him, that now was the time to win her by the death or capture of the murderer of her brother; for she knew his motions, and where he was to be found, indicating to him the place whither she had sent me with his borrowed ensigns.

"To complete her purpose more effectually, she furnished him also with the ensigns of a third lover, named Ariantes, to whom her father had promised her in marriage, on condition of his avenging him on Oringo.

"In the mean time, this Ariantes met and attacked me, taking me by my cognizance for Oringo, and I' yielded myself a prisoner, after little resistance, in the hope of the reward promised by Origilla.

"Lucrino, who was, this while, dispatched by her in pursuit of me, fell in with the real Oringo, and both were desperately wounded in the combat which ensued. Lucrino had, however, strength enough left to master his opposite, and was bringing him away prisoner, when he was met by the father of Origilla, who at first judged him to be Ariantes; but when undeceived on a nearer approach, offered him his daughter in marriage, whom he had pres viously promised to Ariantes on the same conditions, provided he would deliver up his prisoner.

"The offer was scarcely accepted, when Ariantes arrived, bringing in me, disguised in the arms of Oringo; and the whole stratagem was now apparent.

"The clearing up this led to new contests : for Ariantes complained of Lucrino's having taken his bearings; and Oringo thought himself wronged in that his had been usurped by me.

"Now, to wear the ensigns of another is death by our law, unless the penalty be remitted by him who has been offended; and the cause being brought before the king, we were all condemned; Oringo, for having slain (as before told) Corbino, who was a youth scarcely capable of defending himself; Ariantes, for having bargained away the life of another; and Lucrino and myself, for having usurped arms and ensigns, which we were not entitled to wear.

"Origilla was condemned to a yet heavier punishment; to wit, to be hanged up by the hair till she was dead; while we, in the expectation of our sentence, were to assist in the execution of hers; and to keep watch and ward over her, as she wavered in the wind. My lot (for we drew lots to determine the order of our guard) happened to be the first, and I have already slain seven knights, that would have relieved her; whose arms and bearings may be seen fastened to the tree."

The knight had scarcely ended, when the wretched woman gave the lie to his assertions, and denounced him as having slain those he mentioned by treachery, hoping by the show of these trophies to terrify others from attempting to defend her.

Orlando believes the lady, and defies and unhorses Uldano. He is no sooner conquered, than a horn sounds, which a dwarf winds from a tower's top; when another knight takes up the conqueror; and the four concerned are all successively encountered, and dismounted, by Orlando, who now cuts down the damsel, and departs with her seated on his horse's croup.

Thus riding together, and beguiling the way with talk, they descried, in the middle of a meadow, a huge rock of marble cut into steps, and bearing an inscription in letters of gold; when the damsel informs him they are near a notable wonder, which well deserves his examination; since, if he will take the pains of climbing this pile, which is hollow within, he may from the top descry Hell and Paradise, opened to the sight below. Orlando believes the tale, and ascends the steps, when Origilla having possessed herself of Brigliadoro, laughs at him for his folly and departs.

Orlando, now examining the inscription, finds it imports nothing more than that this was the tomb of Ninus, the founder of Nineveh.

Little satisfied with the discovery, and cursing the damsel from the bottom of his soul, he departs on foot, in order to prosecute his adventure.

But here the author closes his first book, with the promise of treating of higher and worthier matters in his second.

Book II.

Argument.

Agramant, king of Africa, assembles his council for advice respecting an intended invasion of France, and is exhorted to seek out Rogero, as necessary to the success of his enterprise. Rinaido, with Astolpho, Iroldo and Prasildo, leaves the camp before Albracca, in search of Orlando, with whom he is impatient to terminate his quarrel. On his way, he falls in with a damsel, in whose behalf he combats with an enchanted man, who plunges with him into a lake, in which they both disappear. Agramant, in the meantime, is unable to find Rogero, and Rodomont of Sarza, one of his vassal kings, determines to undertake the expedition alone. Orlando, who had been dispatched by Angelica on a perilous quest, achieves this and other adventures. She is in the meantime robbed of her magic ring by Brunello, who steals his horse from Sacripant, and her sword from Marphisa. Rodomont, who threatened to invade France alone, embarks for that country in a storm, and makes good his descent. Orlando now falls in with the enchanted man, who had regained the shore after leaving Rinaido below the waves, and a long combat ensues between them on land and under water. Orlando at length vanquishes him, and makes the conquest of Morgana's garden, of which he was the champion. From this Orlando delivers all her prisoners, except Ziliantes, son of Monodontes, her minion; and more especially Rinaldo, to whom he is reconciled. The Christian knights delivered, excepting Orlando, depart to the succour of Charlemagne; but Rinaldo, with his friends, soon falls into a new snare. Orlando, accompanied by Brandimart, returns towards Angelica, in Albracca; but, by the way, encounters Brunello, pursued by Marphisa, and is himself plundered by the fugitive of his sabre and his horn. He is afterwards entrapped by the same spell as the others, and carried prisoner to Damogir, in the empire of Monodontes. This adventure leads to the discovery, that

Brandimart is the eldest son of Monodontes; for whom his younger son, Ziliantes, is also recovered by Orlando, who a second time makes himself master of Morgana. Rinaldo, Astolpho, and the rest, again delivered from prison by him, pursue their way to France; but Astolpho is seduced from his companions by the devices of Alcina. Rinaldo and Rodomont meet in battle in France; but are separated. The invasion of this country is to be attempted by a yet more formidable force than that of Rodomont; for Agramant, having received from Brunello the booty he had made, discovers, by help of the magic ring, the abode of Rogero, and allures him into his service. Orlando, with Angelica, whose covert object is the pursuit of Rinaldo, takes his way to France: she, drinking, however, of the fountain of Disdain, while Rinaldo now drinks of the fountain of Love in the forest of Arden, the two exchange passions; he becomes her lover, and she now mortally detests him, who is involved by his present pursuit of her in a desperate duel with Orlando. Charlemagne, to end the strife, gives Angelica in charge to Namus, duke of Bavaria. Agramant having this while landed in France, pursues the war with various success. The main actions are, as in the first book, diversified with a great variety of episodes.

THE theme, announced as I before stated, begins with the threatened invasion of France; to consult on which, Agramant calls a council of his tributary kings. Here Sobrino strongly opposes the measure; but finding his opposition useless, observes that the only thing which can render it effectual, will be to get possession of Rogero, a youth who is the cousin of Agramant by the mother's side, and now detained a prisoner by the African, Atlantes, on the mountain of Carena. This advice is better listened to than the former, and the council breaks up after it has been adopted, and the king has commanded a search to be prosecuted for him, on whose presence so much appears to depend.

The scene now again shifts to Albracca, from before the walls of which, still besieged by Marphisa, Rinaldo departs in pursuit of his new enemy, Orlando, accompanied by Astolpho, Iroldo, and Prasildo.

Astolpho was at the head of this party when they fell in with a weeping damsel, who, being questioned as to her cause of sorrow, related that, on lately crossing a neighbouring bridge, a wretch had issued from a tower which commanded it, and seized upon her sister that accompanied her, whom he made prisoner, and whipt bitterly; having first stript her, and tied her naked to a cypress. Astolpho immediately places the weeping sister behind him on his horse, and all proceed together to effect the deliverance of the damsel.

The damsel, bridge, tower, and scourging warder are soon descried. Iroldo and Prasildo first encounter the oppressor, but are successively defeated; and the ruffian casts their bodies into a lake, into which the river, bestrid by the bridge, disembogues itself. Rinaldo now attacks him with as little success, and is beat down with an iron mace; but when the conqueror attempts to dispose of him like the others, he makes such violent efforts to free himself, that the savage, being unable to throw him, springs with him into the lake; where they both disappear.

Astolpho remains a long time in affliction upon the banks, but is at last persuaded by the two damsels (for one sister had in the meantime freed the other) to depart.

He accordingly mounts Bayardo, gives Rabican to one of the damsels, and one of the Babylonian knights' horses to the other; and they both, thus mounted, go forth under his guidance.

At this tune, Brandimart (who, it may be remembered, was in Albracca) hearing of Orlando's departure, determines to pursue him.

The same resolution is taken by Gryphon and Aquilant; and these, arriving at the shore, find a castle situated upon the beach, with an open gallery towards the sea. In this, damsels are dancing; and the brothers are informed by two maids, who are passing with hawks upon their fists, that it is their usage to detain every passenger; who is obliged to join in their dance, and to pass a night under their roof.

The brothers consent to submit to this joyous usage, but have soon reason to repent their complaisance. They soon see a damsel approaching upon Brigliadoro, which she had stolen from Orlando, as was told in the former book, and who, being interrogated as to the manner hi which she had become mistress of him, said that he was the horse of a knight (describing his ensigns as those of Orlando) whom she had found dead upon a plain, with the body of a giant by his side.

The two brothers are much distressed by this falsehood, which leaves them little inclination to enjoy the festivities of the castle, in which they had been compelled to join.

To add to their misfortune, they are surprised the ensuing night in their beds; and, having been detained for some days in chains, are, together with the damsel, who had also arrived mounted on Brigliadoro, led forth for execution. As they are however conducting to the place of punishment, a stranger knight is seen approaching; but here the author breaks off, and carries his readers back to the war before Albracca.

Marphisa had now encountered and worsted every one of the defenders of Angelica, in an attack which they made upon her camp, when she was assailed by Sacripant, who had hitherto been confined to the fortress from the effects of a former wound.

A desperate combat ensues, in which the Circassian is much assisted by the speed and docility of his horse Frontilatte. In the heat of this a courier brings him news of the invasion of his kingdom by Mandricardo, the. son of Agricaiu As he and Marphisa, however, cannot agree upon the conditions of a truce, this occasions but a short interruption of the duel; which is at last only broken off by the author, that he may give some account of the search made for Rogero, in consequence of what was determined at the council of Agramant.

The emissary of the king returns, reporting the inutility of his journey, made through the mountain of Carena, and Rodomont, enraged at the delay, sets out with his own forces for the invasion of France. In the mean time Agramant is assured that Rogero is upon Mount Carena; though the garden, where he is confined, is invisible; and that the possession of Angelica's ring would enable him to succeed in his enterprise.

Agramant now promises a kingdom to whoever shall obtain for him this prize, and the theft is confidently promised by a dwarf, who is entitled Brunello.

This while, Orlando, robbed by the damsel of Brigliadoro, was plodding upon his way a-foot : when he one day fell in with an escort of armed men, leading two knights as prisoners, whom he immediately recognized for Gryphon and Aquilant, and the damsel who had carried off his courser.

The escort was, it seems, carrying off these to be devoured by the serpent of the garden of Orgagna; but Orlando immediately routs the guard, and sets the prisoners at liberty.

He has scarcely looked the damsel in the face, when he forgets the wrongs he has received; and Gryphon, who had exchanged hearts with her, almost at sight, is yet more fascinated by her graces. Orlando observing this, under some pretence sends the two brothers away, that he may keep her to himself; and sitting down by her on the grass, begins to woo her with such courtesy as he can.

While he is thus engaged, another damsel approaches on a white palfrey, who warns Orlando of impending danger, and informs him he is close to the garden of Orgagna. Orlando is delighted at the intelligence, and entreats her to inform him how he is to procure admittance.

She promises him full instructions; and, as the first of these, tells him he must keep himself chaste for three days, previous to attempting the adventure, if he would preserve himself from being devoured by the dragon, who guards the gate. She then says she will give him a book, in which he will find painted the garden and all it contains, together with the palace of the false enchantress, which she had only entered the day before, for the purpose of executing a magic work in which she was engaged.

This, which was the manufacture of a sword, capable of cutting through even enchanted substances, she only pursued on moonless nights.

The object of this labour was the destruction of a knight of the west, hight Orlando; who, she had read in the book of Fate, was destined to demolish her garden. To this, the damsel adds, that the garden can only be entered at sunrise; and, having presented him with a book of instructions, departs.

Orlando, who finds he must delay his enterprize till the next morning, now lies down, and is soon asleep. In the mean time, Origilla, who was still with him, meditated her escape, in order to rejoin Gryphon; and yielding to the impulse of her evil nature, was about to slay Orlando with his own sword, which she had drawn for the purpose. Afraid, however, to execute her design, she mounts Brigliadoro, and gallops off, carrying away Durindana.

Orlando wakes, in such indignation as may be supposed, on the discovery of the theft; but, like a good knight and true, is not to be diverted from his enterprise. He tears off a huge branch of elm to supply the place of his sword, and, the sun rising, takes his way towards the eastern gate, where the dragon was on his watch.

This he slays by repeated blows upon the spine; but finds that the wall of the enchanted garden, which he had entered, was closed upon him. Looking round him, he saw a fair fountain of water, which overflowed into a river, and in the centre of the fountain was a figure, on whose forehead was written,

"The stream which waters violet and rose,
From hence to the enchanted palace flows."

Following the banks of this flowery stream, and rapt in the delights of the delicious garden, Orlando arrives at the palace, and entering it, finds the mistress, clad in white, and with a crown of gold upon her head, in the act of viewing herself in the surface of the fatal sword.

He surprises her before she can escape, deprives her of the weapon, and holding her fast by her long hair, which floated behind, threatens her with immediate death if she does not instruct him in the means of retreat.

Falerina, however, was firm of purpose, and refused. Hence Orlando, being unable to move her either by threats or kindness, was under the necessity of binding her to a beech. Having thus secured his prisoner, he renewed his questions, but she still refused to point out the gate of the garden.

He now bethinks him of his book, and consulting it, finds there is an entrance to the south but that it is watched by a bull, with one horn of iron, and another of flame.

Moreover, before arriving at this, there is another impediment: a lake is to be passed, pregnant with new danger; but to provide against this, he is instructed by his book. According to its directions,

He, still his path pursuing, gathers posies
Of flowers, which every where about him spring,
And filling well his casque and ears with roses,
Lists if he hears the birds in green-wood sing :
He sees the gaping beak, the swelling throat,
And ruffled plumes, but cannot catch a note.

Having thus proved the force of his defence, he proceeds towards the lake, which was small but deep; and so clear and tranquil, that the eye could penetrate to the bottom.

He is no sooner arrived upon the banks, than the waters are seen to gurgle; and a syren, rising midway out of the pool, sings so sweetly, that birds and beasts troop to the water-side, attracted by her song. Of this the count hears nothing; but feigning to yield to the charm, sinks down beside the water; from which the syren issues with the intent to accomplish his destruction. Orlando, however, seizes her by the hair, and, while singing yet louder (song being her only defence), cuts off her head, and (so instructed by the book) stains himself all over with her blood.

Having done this as a protection against the horns of the bull, and taken the roses from his helmet and ears, he proceeds towards the southern gate.

Here he is encountered by the bull, whose horn of iron he severs at a stroke. His horn of flame was however yet left, and by this Orlando, but for the virtue of the syren's blood, would have been consumed. Guarded by this, he pursues his advantage, and at last slaughters his enemy. The bull is, however, no sooner slain, than the gate, of which he is the guardian, disappears, the wall closes, and Orlando again finds himself a prisoner, without the means of escape.

Again resorting to his book, he finds that another river, running westward, leads to a gate formed of jewels, which is kept by an enchanted ass.

Taking his course towards this, he arrives at a tree of surprising height, and again consulting his book, razes off his crest, and makes a penthouse of his shield for the protection of his sight. Covering himself with it, he advances with his eyes fixed upon the ground, towards the miraculous tree.

On approaching it, a harpy with a beautiful female head, and crowned with strangely coloured plumes, flutters out from the branches, and hovering above the count, squirts her ordure at his head. This is fortunately protected by his shield, on which it hisses like boiling oil. Orlando, distracted by the yells of the harpy, is often tempted to raise his eyes : he however perseveres in keeping them fixed to the ground till he is near the tree, when he falls, as if blinded by the burning liquor. The bird now swoops to the ground, and having darted her talons into his breast-plate, attempts to drag him towards the trunk. The count sees his time is come, and dispatches her with a back-handed stroke of his sword.

The harpy demolished, he re-adjusted his crest, the gift of Angelica, braced his shield anew, and took his way towards the western gate. Nothing was ever seen more beautiful than this, with respect to the materials, or the workmanship. Nor was the animal who kept it less extraordinary; being an ass, armed with scales of gold, and ears of such length and strength, as to be able to seize, and drag to himself by the aid of them, whatever was within his reach; his tail cut like a trenchant sword, and his bray made the forest tremble.

Though his golden scales had resisted all other weapons, they were not impenetrable by Orlando's steel, and he smote off his head at a blow.

A strange wonder followed; the earth swallowed the carcase of the ass, this gate too disappeared, and the walls again closed upon Orlando.

He is now directed by his instructions to a a northern entrance, and, strong in patience, proceeds in this direction. On his way thither he sees a table spread in the wilderness. He is tempted by the viands; but recurring to the book, is informed of his danger, and refrains.

From this he learns that a faun lay conceale amongst the neighbouring thorns and roses, provided with a chain, with which she snared whoever tasted of the banquet. She fled from Orlando on his approaching her haunt, dragging after her a serpent's tail, till then concealed, which was as loathsome as her face was lovely. Being overtaken, she made no defence and was slaughtered at a blow.

The count now arrives at the northern gate, which he finds guarded by a giant. Orlando had so often been engaged with enemies of this description, that he thought little of the combat in which he was going to engage. In effect, his expectations were in part justified, as he slew his adversary. This was, however, but the beginning of his labour; for, from the blood of the slaughtered enemy sprang a fire, and from this issued two other giants yet fiercer than the first. Orlando sees that to spill the blood of these, would be but to multiply his foes, and accordingly, changing his mode of proceeding, grapples with one of the two in the hopes of squeezing him to death. He is, however, still interrupted by the other, before he can accomplish his purpose; and at last sees the necessity of separating them.

To effect this, he feigns to fly, but the giants, instead of pursuing, return to keep guard over the enchanted gate. If, however, Orlando was disappointed in his hope of dividing them, his stratagem was productive of another advantage. He saw the chain lying on the ground, which was spread for his destruction by the faun. Returning with this, he nooses the giants and then again recurs to the book for his future proceedings.

This informs him, that the total destruction of the garden (the task imposed by Angelica) can only be accomplished by tearing off a certain branch of a lofty tree, in which was involved the destiny of this fairy creation.

According to the rules which he received, he returned through a spacious valley towards the palace, passing Falerina, whom he had left fastened to the beech. He soon descries the fatal tree, which is of an immeasurable height : while the stem, even at the bottom, is no more than a palm in girt.

No thicker; but from this close branch and spray
Bristled, whence foliage green and narrow grew.
The leaves which died and sprouted every day,
Conceal'd within sharp pointed thorns from view:
Apples of gold the loaded twigs display;
Apples in form, but burnish'd gold in hue,
Suspended from small stalks, so slight in show,
The man had periled life who walked below.

To obviate this danger (and we are afterwards told that the fruit was as large as the human head), Orlando forms a sort of grating of boughs of trees, and, under cover of this, proceeds towards the tree, amidst a shower of the golden apples, which fall, loosened by the vibration of the soil beneath his feet. Having reached it, he severs the trunk close to the root, and every thing is instantly involved in darkness.

The cloud at length clears away, and the sun shines forth upon a wild landscape; where no vestige is to be seen of the garden, or trace of the adventure, except in the appearance of the fairy Falerina, who remains in the middle of the wilderness, fastened to the beech.

Her tone is now changed, and she entreats Orlando's mercy, assuring him that many lives depend upon the preservation of hers. She explains herself by saying, that she had constructed the garden and a neighbouring snare in a bridge over a torrent, in order to be revenged on a knight called Ariantes, and an infamous woman of the name of Origilla, who, though many had fallen into her toils, had both hitherto escaped.

"Many," pursues the fairy, " were entrapped in my garden, and yet more at the bridge; and here it was that I took a certain enchantress, daughter of king Galaphron, who by some secret means escaped, and effected the deliverance of her fellow prisoners. Many more, however, have been taken since, and all these will perish, if you are resolved on my destruction." Orlando immediately promised her life, upon her pledging herself for the deliverance of the captives.

With this view they proceed together, towards the bridge; but the author snaps this thread, to take up that of the story of Albracca.

Here Sacripant and Marphisa were left engaged in a single combat, which was still continued with mutual animosity; while Angelica, surrounded by a group of warriors, sate contemplating the fight from the ramparts of the citadel. While the attention of all was thus engaged, Brunello, who (it will be remembered) had undertaken to steal Angelica's ring, arrived beneath the walls of Albracca, scaled the rock and walls of the fortress, while the crowd was watching the duel, and disputing on its probable result, approached the princess unobserved, and, slipping the ring from her finger, escaped amid the confusion which followed.

Having descended safely to the ground, and swam a water by which the citadel was surrounded, the dwarf perceived that the two combatants had separated for an interval of repose, and immediately meditated a new exercise of his art. With this view, he approached Sacripant, who, absorbed in an amorous reverie, sate apart, upon his courser, and having first loosened the girths, and supported the saddle by a piece of wood, withdrew the horse from under him.[23]

Marphisa, who was at a little distance, witnessed this with wonder, and, before she recovered from her astonishment, was herself plundered of her sword. Marphisa is no sooner aware of the theft, than she pursues the robber; but he, mounted upon Frontilatte, his new acquisition, soon distances the pursuer.

---

[23] The reader will recollect the imitation of this absurd incident in "Don Quixote," whoso squire's ass, Dapple, is stolen in a similar manner.

While Angelica, who felt her misfortune yet more than the others, is in despair at the loss of her treasure, an alarm is given by the warder, who reports the arrival of a new army before Albracca. This was a Turkish force, led by Caramano, brother of Torindo, one of the princes who had been seized and imprisoned by Truffaldino, and who, having refused to enter into the engagement to which the others agreed, on his delivering them from durance, now brought this brother against Albracca.

Angelica's last hopes of deliverance rest upon Gradasso; who, it seems, was her relation, and who was meditating anew the invasion of France. Hence Sacripant undertakes a secret embassy to this prince, with the view of soliciting his succour.

Rodomont, this while, who was too impatient to wait for Agramanfs attack upon Charlemagne, had already sailed for France. A tremendous storm wrecked his fleet upon the coast of that kingdom; but he, landing with such force as the tempest had left him, made good his footing, and routed the Christians in more engagements than one: though the balance at last turned in their favour.

Previous, however, to this, Gano, or Ganelon, (as he is sometimes called) enters into a traitorous correspondence with Marsilius, whom he invites into France.

While great events are preparing in this quarter, the author resumes the story of Orlando, who was journeying with Falerina towards the bridge, where so many prisoners were entrapped. On their way thither, however, they arrived at a yet more perilous pass : this was the bridge, and lake into which the felon warrior leaped with Rinaldo in his arms. Falerina, enchantress as she was, turned pale at the sight of this place, and cursed the hour in which they had taken the road which conducted them thither; informing Orlando that they were approaching a snare, laid by Morgana; who plotted revenge against a knight who had destroyed many of her spells, and set at nought her riches and her power.

For this purpose she had formed the lake; and selected, as a defender of the pass, a man named Arridano, a churl of the most ferocious and pitiless character she could find. Him she had clothed in invulnerable arms, and charmed in such a manner, that his strength always increased in a six-fold proportion to that of the adversary with whom he was matched. Hence, no one had hitherto escaped from the contest; since, such was his strength and power of endurance, that he could breathe freely under water. Hence, having grappled with a knight, and sunk with him to the bottom of the lake, he returned, bearing his arms in triumph to the top.

While Falerina is explaining the danger of the enterprise, Orlando sees Rinaldo's arms, erected in form of a trophy, amongst other spoils made by the villain; and forgetting their late quarrel, determines upon revenging his friend. A desperate contest ensues between the churl and the knight, during which Falerina flies. The combatants (as in the case of Rinaldo) both grapple, and sink together in the water. Arrived at the bottom, Orlando finds himself in another world, upon a dry meadow, with the lake overhead, through which shone the beams of our sun; the meadow being on all sides surrounded by a crystal wall. Here the battle was renewed, and in this Orlando had an advantage, which none had hitherto possessed. Besides that lie was himself invulnerable, he was now in possession of the sword, tempered by Falerina, against which no spells could avail. Thus armed, and countervailing the strength of his adversary by his superior skill and activity, he had the good fortune to lay him dead upon the field.

Orlando having slain his foe, discovers a gate in the crystal wall; and having passed through a dark labyrinth, comes at last where it is lighted by a carbuncle, whose lustre was equal to that of day. This discovered to his view a river little less than twenty-yards over, and beyond this was seen a field as thickly covered with precious stones as the sky is full of stars.

Over this was thrown a bridge, only half a palm wide, and at each end was stationed an iron figure with a mace. Orlando no sooner attempted to pass this, than the figures smote upon it, and it was instantly engulphed in the stream. Orlando however, being resolved to accomplish the adventure or perish in the attempt, leapt the river and arrived in the field, which contained the treasures of the fairy.

When he had arrived at the other extremity of this, he entered a building, where he beheld the likeness of a king, surrounded by his peers, and encompassed by all the pomp and magnificence of royalty. The monarch appeared to be seated at a banquet, with a naked sword suspended over his head, and on the table before him was a live coal, supported on a golden lily, which gave light to the apartment. On his left stood a figure with a bended bow in guise of one who waits the crossing of the stag; and on the right, the form of one, who, from his likeness to the king, appeared to be his brother, and who bore in one hand a writing illustrative of the vanity of his worldly pursuits.

The troubled countenance of the king seemed to bear witness to the truth of the inscription; and Orlando, having satisfied his curiosity, departed through the door opposite to that by which he had entered. He was however no sooner out of the apartment, than all was darkness.

After wandering for some time at random, he bethought himself of the coal, which was burning before the king, and returned in order to take it. He had however no sooner laid his hand upon this, than the archer let fly his arrow, which extinguished it, and night followed. This was rendered terrible by an earthquake, which shook the world to its centre. The earthquake at last ceased, the light rekindled of itself, and all was as before. Again Orlando issued through the dark passage, again was compelled to return in search of the coal, and again witnessed the same effect.

A third attempt was more successful : he intercepted the arrow with his shield, and carried off the light in safety. Using this as a lamp, Orlando arrived where the way divided; and turning to the left, instead of the right (which would have conducted him out of the building) took the road which led to the dungeons of Morgana. Here were imprisoned Rinaldo, Dudon, Brandimart, and others who had fallen into the power of Morgana; but the count did not immediately arrive at their place of confinement. Still guiding himself by his light, he came to a cleft in the rock, through which he passed into a flowery meadow, planted with trees covered with fruit and flowers, and full of all imaginable delights.

In the middle of this was a fountain, and fast by it lay Morgana asleep; a lady of a lovely aspect, dressed in white and vermilion garments; her forehead well furnished with hair, but with scarcely any behind.

While Orlando stood in silence, contemplating her beauty, he heai'd a voice exclaim, "Seize the fairy by the forelock if thou hopest fair success;" Orlando turning, and advancing in the direction from which the voice came, discovered a prison of crystal in which he beheld the captives of Morgana.

At the sight of these, he raised his sabre to smite the wall; but was advertised by a female prisoner that all attempts to release them would only be productive of new misery to those he sought to benefit, unless he could take Morgana herself, and force from her the keys of their prison-house.

Thus admonished, he returned towards the fountain. But the fairy, who was awake and risen, was now dancing round its border with the lightness of a leaf, and timing her steps to the following song :
    "Who in this world would wealth and treasure share,
    "Honour, delight, and state, and what is best,
    "Quick let him catch me by the lock of hair
    "Which flutters from my forehead, and be blest;
    "But let him not the proffered good forbear,
    "Nor, till he seize the fleeting blessing, rest.
    "For present loss is sought in vain to-morrow,
    "And the deluded wretch is left in sorrow."
The fairy, however, no sooner set eyes on the count, than she bounded off, and fled from the flowery meadow over a high and inhospitable mountain. Orlando pursued her through thorns and rocks, though the sky, on her gaining this dreary scene, became overcast, and he was assailed by tempest, lightning and hail.

While Orlando thus pursues, enveloped in storm, a pale and meagre woman issues from a cave, armed with a whip, and treading close upon the pursuer, scourges him, till his skin is raised in furrows. She infbrms him, while she inflicts this discipline, that she is Penitence, and sent to punish him for having neglected to seize Morgana, when he found her sleeping by the fountain. Orlando, determined to resist this chastisement, turns upon his tormentor; but might as well seek to wound the wind. Convinced at last of the shadowy nature of his persecutor, and observing that Morgana gained upon him, while he was thus hopelessly engaged, he determines to pursue the fairy without being diverted by the molestation of Penitence.

Chasing Morgana, then, over rock and hill, he mode sundry snatches at her white and vermilion garments, which still eluded his grasp. On the fairy, however, turning her. head for an instant, he profited by the chance, and seized her by the forelock. In an instant the tempest ceased, the sky became serene, and Penitence retreated into her cave.

Orlando now demanded of Morgana the keys of her dungeon; and the fairy, feigning a complacent aspect, told him that these were at his disposal; entreating him, though he should free all her other prisoners, to leave her a youthful son of Monodontes, who was her darling. Orlando consented to this, and the fairy delivered up a key of silver, bidding him be cautious in the use of it; since, to break the lock, would be to involve himself and all, in inevitable destruction; a caution which gave the count room for long meditation, and led him to consider

How few amid the suitors, who importune

The dame, know how to guide the keys of Fortune.

Keeping the fairy still fast by the forelock, Orlando proceeded towards the prison, turned the key without occasioning the mischief apprehended, and delivered the prisoners.

Amongst these were Brandimart, Rinaldo, and all the knights, baptized or infidel, who had been taken at the bridge. The only unhappy person amid this joyous band was Ziliantes, the minion of Morgana. This youth remained behind weeping;

and time will come, says the author, when Orlando will repent of having yielded to the entreaties of the fairy.

The others, now delivered from their captivity, together with Orlando, ascending a lofty stair" issued into the field of treasure, where was to be seen the king and his court, all composed of the richest materials in the world. Rinaldo, on finding himself amid this mass of wealth, could not resist the temptation of seizing a gold seat that stood in his way, which, he observed, would feed his hungry garrison of Mont Albano. This he was bearing off, notwithstanding the remonstrances of Orlando, when a violent wind blew him back as often as he approached the gate, by which they were retiring. Rinaldo at length yielded to necessity, rather than to the entreaties of his comrades, and cast away his prize. All now climbing another immeasurable stair, ascended into the upper world, and found themselves in the field decorated with their arms.

Here each knight resumed his own; and all except the paladins and their friends, separated, as their inclinations or duty prompted. It was now that Dudon informed the cousins that he had been made prisoner by Morgana, when in the discharge of an — embassy to them from Charlemagne, who called upon them to return to the defence of Christendom. Orlando is too much fascinated by Angelica, to obey this summons; and, followed by the faithful Brandimart, returns towards Albracca. Rinaldo, accompanied by Dudon, Iroldo and Prasildo, takes his way towards the west.

These, though unprovided with horses, (for their coursers were lost at the bridge,) went laughing and talking on their way. Their journey was without adventures till the sixth day, when they heard a horn sound from a neighbouring castle. From this they were divided by a river, and near the opposite bank was a small bark, with a damsel in the stern, who proflercd them a passage.

Arrived on the other shore, she tells them they must account for this with the warder, who was then approaching. This was an old man mounted on a heavy steed, and surrounded by a numerous escort. He informs the knights, that they are upon the territory of the king Monodontes, from which they will not be suffered to depart, before they have rendered him a day's service. This was to avenge him of a certain enemy named Balisardo, at once a giant and enchanter, who kept a bridge, flanked with towers, near the mouth of the river which they had crossed, and who had put many scorns upon that monarch and those who travelled to his realm.

Nothing more agreeable could have been proposed to the warriors, and they reimbark in the damsel's skiff for the purpose of seeking the necromancer.

The event of the combat was, however, very different from what they had anticipated. Encountering the giant singly, they all became the victims of his enchantments, and were cast into his dungeons, already peopled with illustrious knights, amongst whom' was Astolpho of England.

This prince, in company with the two damsels before mentioned, had gone about the world, with Bayardo and Rabican, weeping the loss of Rinaldo, whom he saw go to the bottom of the enchanted lake with Arridano. Wandering thence, he had arrived on the same spot where Rinaldo and his comrades afterwards found themselves; like them he had ferried the river in die damsel's boat, like them, had been dispatched against Balisardo; and, like them, had been made prisoner by the wizard, who ensnared him, under" the form of a damsel.

In the mean time, Orlando, who had parted company with Rinaldo, and the rest, was returning, with Brandimart, towards Albracca On his way thither he, to his surprise, saw Marphisa in chase of Brunello, and contemp — , lating the two, was himself robbed of his horn, and Balisarda.

As both he and Brandimart were on foot, to chase the robber was useless; leaving, therefore, Marphisa still in pursuit, the two warriors proceeded on their way. Pursuing this, they too arrived at die same ferry as Rinaldo had, and there found two damsels assailing each other with reproaches, the one in a boat, and the other on horseback. Orlando immediately recognized the latter for Origilla, who had stolen Brigliadoro and Durindana, previous to his entering the garden of Orgagna. His resentment, however, was forgotten on seeing her; and he received her again into his company, embarking, as the others had done, for the adventure of Balisardo.

In this his usual fortune deserted him, and having been vanquished by the enchantments of the giant, he was cast on board a miserable prison-ship, in order to be transported to some distant dungeons.

From this he is, however, delivered by the valour of Brandimart[24], who slays the giant, and rescues Orlando from captivity. The two champions now interrogate the master of the prison-ship; who tells them that the wizard-giant was the instrument of a certain king, called Monodontes, who dwelt in Damogir, an island situated in the ocean; where he had amassed riches, which surpassed the imagination to conceive. As, something is always wanting to the completion of human happiness, this prince was miserable in the loss of his two only sons, the first of whom was carried off, in his childhood, by a slave of the name of Bardino, and the second taken and imprisoned by a fairy named Morgana, who was said to be enamoured of the youth.

The ship-master, pursuing his story, stated that the fairy had offered to surrender the stripling to his father, upon his putting her in possession of a certain knight, entitled Orlando, with whom she was at enmity, on account of his having destroyed her enchantments. This the necromancer, overcome by Brandimart, had offered to effect for Monodontes, but had never succeeded, though he had crowded his dungeons with champions; amongst whom were Rinaldo, Astolpho, Dudon, Gryphon and Aquilant, and others, too many to mention.

---

[24] The reader will have remarked that a vein of allegory, more or less apparent, runs through the whole of the romance. This observation will, perhaps, serve to explain the defeat of Orlando, and the subsequent triumph of Brandimart. Orlando, by his love of vice, as figured in Origilla, has derogated from his natural self, and forfeited the protection of Providence, while Brandimart, the model of purity and constancy, is proof against all the powers of hell.

Orlando listened to the narration in silence : then, after some secret conference with the ship-master, bade him make sail for Damogir, as he and Brandimart were now masters of the vessel, for he was minded to put this Orlando into the hands of Monodontes. He obeys his command, and the ship, after traversing the ocean, arrives with them at the island.

Here the proposal was renewed by the knights, and accepted by Monodontes; who, waiting the accomplishment of their promise, lodged them in a magnificent palace near his own. Here too was guested the infamous Origilla, who was privy to Orlando's design. She having her mind entirely set upon Gryphon, who (it will be remembered) was amongst the prisoners of Monodontes, and thinking she was possessed of sure means of delivering him, secretly presented herself before the king, and informed him that Orlando was in his power.

As the covenanted reward of her service, Monodontes ordered Gryphon to be delivered up to her; and he refusing freedom, unless Aquilant was at the same time freed, both were set at liberty, and departed with Origilla.

To take Orlando was a more difficult enterprise; but this was accomplished through the means of a potion, by which both he and Brandimart were put to sleep, and, while stupefied by the liquor, lodged in the dungeons of Monodontes.' In the solitude of their prison Orlando converts Brandimart to the Christian faith; and this knight, who appears to be the type of friendship and virtuous love, upon the guards of the monarch coming in search of Orlando, announces himself as the person sought for, and as such presents himself to Monodontes.

This monarch tells Brandimart, whom he imagines to be Orlando, that he seeks the liberation of his son Ziliantes; and as he knows no method of obtaining him from the fairy, but by such a sacrifice, is reluctantly compelled . to offer hun in exchange for the royal captive. To which Brandimart replies, that if he only seeks this, he may obtain his end without such a breach of hospitality, as his comrade is ready to descend to the dungeons of Morgana, where he has already been, and rescue him by force.

That in the meantime he will remain as his hostage, and if he whom he is to free does not, within a month, return with Ziliantes, the king can, at the worst, accomplish the deliverance of his son, by giving him up (the king believing him to be Orlando) to the vengeance of Morgana.

Monodontes accedes to this proposal, and the real Orlando is suffered to depart.

In the meantime Brandimart, always under the name of Orlando, remains for some time a prisoner at large; when the secret is discovered, through the indiscretion of Astolpho, and Monodontes in fury orders Brandimart to be cast into a dungeon, preparatory to his expiating his imposture by death. Orlando this while is bound upon his adventure, and arriving at the lake formerly kept by Arridano, finds upon its banks a beautiful lady weeping over a dead dragon.

While Orlando contemplates this spectacle with surprise, the lady snatches up the dragon in her arms, and embarks with it in a Little pinnace, which was moored hard by. She now loosens from the shore, sets her sail, and having reached the middle of the lake, sinks to the bottom with her enchanted barque.

Orlando was yet absorbed in wonder at what he had witnessed, when another damsel arrived upon the bank, mounted on a palfrey, and accompanied by a single sergeant, who called upon the count by name, and expressed the greatest pleasure at his sight.

This damsel was no other than Flordelis, the lady-love of Brandimart; the damsel of the barque, it will be easily divined, was Morgana.

This fairy, upon the departure of Orlando from her enchanted garden, transformed Ziliantes, by the aid of certain witcheries, into a dragon, meaning that he should supply the place of Arridano and keep the avenues of her territory. Whether, however, from some error in her enchantments or other cause, the transformation was no sooner completed than the youth uttered a shriek and expired. Hence the fairy, distracted with her loss, had embarked with him in the pinnace, and descended to the bottom of the lake, hi the hope of re-animating him in her world below.

As soon as Flordelis, who was immediately recognised by the count, had set eyes upon him, she conjured him to lend her his assistance; and, that he might understand for what purpose, entreated him to listen to her story, which she began in the following words.

"I was wandering in search of Brandimart, when I fell in with the sergeant, whom you see with me; and who, by a strange fortune, turned out to be one who was also in search of him. His story was yet more extraordinary than the accident which brought us together, and is the cause of my present distress. He informed me that he was formerly a slave of the king Monodontes, and named Bardino; who, to avenge himself upon the monarch for some wrong, conveyed away from him his eldest son, and sold him to the lord of the Svlvan Tower; who conceived such fondness for him, that he brought him up as his son, and dying, left him his possessions.

"His love of arms, however, carried him away from the Tower, of which he had made Bardino castellan; and this was attacked by a neighbour named Rupardo, in his absence, with such forces as rendered a defence hopeless. Under these circumstances Bardino, had cast lots to learn the fate of Brandimart, and found that he was prisoner to Morgana. Hence it is," pursued the damsel, " that I entreat you to lend your assistance to recover him from her power."

Orlando related in return what had since happened to Brandimart, and, lastly, how he had left him in the power of Monodontes, meaning to redeem him, by the recovery of Ziliantes, from the prisons of Morgana.

The damsel heard Orlando's recital with gratitude, and, throwing herself on her knees, prayed devoutly for the success of his undertaking.

He immediately entered upon his adventure. Descending by the entrance, through which he had formerly ascended into the upper air, and which he remembered, though concealed by briars and thorns, he again traversed the field of treasure, and saw the golden seat, lying in the very place where Rinaldo had been obliged to abandon it.

Thus pursuing his old path, he came upon Morgana near the fountain, where he had formerly found her disporting herself.

She was this time engaged in a very different occupation, and was caressing Ziliantes, who had now resumed the human form, but remained yet pale, and terrified by the effects of the metamorphose. The count does not again neglect his opportunity, but, seizing the fairy by the forelock, compels her to abandon her prisoner. Orlando returning into light with Ziliantes by the ancient staircase, finds Flordelis yet engaged in prayer, and now all journeying to the coast, which was near, and embarking upon the ocean, arrive safely at Damogir.

The delight of Monodontes at the recovery of his two sons, when he had despaired of even retrieving Ziliantes, may be easily imagined: king and people become Christians; Rinaldo, Astolpho, Dudon, and the other prisoners are set at liberty; all is festivity, and the offence of Bardino is forgiven, in consequence of his subsequent attachment to Brandimart. To complete the general joy, a lady arrives at this period, who is recognized as the daughter of Monodontes and the damsel of the golden apples.

But human life is chequered by light and shade. The long continued festivities of Damogir are broken in upon by Dudon the Dane, who reminds the princes of their obligation to hurry to the defence of Christendom.

Rinaldo and all the Franks obey the summons, with the exception of Orlando; who, accompanied by Brandimart, his inseparable companion, returns towards Albracca. In the meantime Rinaldo, Iroldo, Prasildo, and the others, with Astolpho in the midst, armed with his lance of gold, set forward on their return to France.

Travelling thus, north about, into Europe, the knights found themselves one morning in front of a beautiful castle and garden on the sea-shore. This was the domain of Alcina, sister of Morgana, and queen of the Atarberi. The fay herself was standing on the beach, and amusing herself with taking fish, which she inveigled by her enchantments.

She herself was ensnared by the beauties of Astolpho, whom she invited to pass into a neighbouring island, in order to hear the music of a syren who frequented it.

Astolpho crosses on horseback into the island, which lay close to the shore; but this is in motion as soon as he reaches it, and proves to be a large whale, which was a minister of the fairy. Rinaldo and Dudon instantly swim off to his assistance, but the horse of Dudon sinking with his rider, Rinaldo is . compelled to swim Bayardo to the relief of the Dane, whom he succeeds in bringing to shore.. Meantime the whale floats out of sight, and a terrible tempest obscures both sky and ocean. —

To succour Astolpho' was now' impossible, I and the confederated champions continued their journey to the westward.

Pursuing this, they at last arrived at Buda in Hungary, whence the king of that country was dispatching his son Ottachiero with a large army to the succour of Charlemagne. Delighted with the arrival of Rinaldo, he placed his son and troops under this conduct, and these having, after long and distant marches, united themselves with the troops of Desiderius king of Lombardy, passed the Genovese Alps, and poured down into Provence.

The confederate armies had not marched many days through this gay tract, before they heard a crash of drums and trumpets behind the hills, which spoke the conflict between the paynims, led by Rodomont, and the Christian forces.

Rinaldo, witnessing from a mountain the prowess of Rodomont, leaves his troops in charge of his friends, and gallops towards him with "his lance in the rest. The impulse is irresistible, and Rodomont is unhorsed. Rinaldo, however, in a high spirit of chivalry, gallops back to the hill from which he had descended, secures Bayardo amongst the baggage, and returns to pursue the combat with his former antagonist on foot.

During this interval the battle had become general, the Hungarians were routed by Rodomont, and Rinaldo, on his return, had the mortification to find that Ottachiero was. wounded, and Dudon a prisoner.

He now again engages Rodomont; when in the midst of their strife, a new sound of drums and trumpets was heard, and die army of Charlemagne was descried advancing in battalia.

Rodomont, who had in the meantime mounted the horse of Dudon, leaves Rinaldo, who was on foot, and gallops to the attack of the enemy. A desperate battle ensues, but night separates the combatants.

Rodomont now thinks only of Rinaldo, and deceived by a false report, sets off in pursuit of him towards the forest of Arden.

Rinaldo, however, having this time gone in search of Bayardo, was returning towards the field upon that courser, when he fell in with the Saracens, engaged in carrying aboard their ships the plunder, and the prisoners made in battle. Some of these had already sailed for Africa with Dudon, while Rinaldo, still seeking Rodomont, makes a tremendous carnage among the rest.

He at last learns that his adversary, following a false scent, is gone towards Merlin's fountain, in the forest of Arden, when he quits the pursuit of the Saracens, in order to follow him.

Rodomont was in the meantime far advanced upon his way, when he fell in with a strange cavalier, that proved to be Ferrau, who had, it seems, returned to France, in search of Angelica. The two knights mixing in conversation, their talk, according to the practice of chivalry, turned upon love, when Ferrau spoke of Doralice, daughter of Stordilano, king of Granada, as a lady to whom he had been a suitor. Rodomont, kindling at this, avowed his passion for her, declared he would bear with no rival in his love, and bade him resign all pretensions to her, or take his ground and defend himself. Ferrau replied, that he had loved her and left her; but that he would now love her in his despite.

A duel ensues, but the author leaves the knights engaged, in order to pursue the story of Rinaldo. He, still seeking his pursuer, Rodomont, misses him, whilst he is engaged in combat with Ferrau; and wandering into a sylvan lawn, in the middle of the forest of Arden, is surprised by the vision of a beautiful child, dancing naked, with three damsels, as naked and as beautiful as himself. While he is lost in admiration at the sight, the child approaches him, and smiting on his helmet with a bunch of roses and lilies, strikes him from his horse. He is no sooner down than he is seized by the dancers, by whom he is dragged about and scourged with flowers till he falls into a swoon. While he is yet absorbed in this, one of the group approaches him, who says her name is Pasiphae; that his punishment is the consequence of his rebellion against that power, before whom every thing bends; and that there is but one remedy that can heal the wounds which have been inflicted; and this is, to drink of the waters of Love.

Rinaldo, sore and faint, drags himself into the neighbouring wood, and being parched with thirst, drinks greedily, and almost unconsciously, of a spring which he finds there. After repeated draughts of the water, which is sweet to the taste, but bitter at the heart, he recovers his strength and recollection, and finds himself in the same place where Angelica had formerly awakened him with a rain of flowers, and whence he had fled in contempt of her courtesy.

His remembrance of the scene is followed by the recognition of his crime; and, repenting bitterly of his ingratitude, he leaps upon Bayardo with the intention of following Angelica to India, and soliciting his pardon at her feet. He has not ridden far with this intention, when he beholds, at a distance, a damsel mounted upon a palfrey, attended by a cavalier who bore a burning mountain for his device : but, before explaining who were the damsel and knight, the author returns to Marphisa, lately left in pursuit of Brunello.

She had now hunted him for fifteen days. Her horse had sunk under her during the chase; and she had cast away her arms, to be the better able to pursue him.

Her pains were thrown away. Brunello arrived before her at the sea-side, and finding a vessel ready to sail, embarked, and arrived at Biserta, in Africa. Here he found Agramant, who was impatient for the ring, which was to foil the enchantments of

Atlantes and to put Rogero into his hands. The dwarf, now kneeling be-; fore die king, related his story, and presented him with the ring of Angelica, and the horn stolen from Orlando; when Agramant, delighted at the success of his mission, crowned him, in recompense, king of Tingitana.

All are now anxious to go in quest of Rogero, nor will Brunello be left behind. The cavalcade accordingly departs, and having traversed the Great Desert, arrives at the mountain of Carena.

At the bottom of this was a fruitful and well-wooded plain, watered by a large river, which traversed it in its way to the sea; and .from this plain was descried a beautiful garden on the mountain-top, which contained the mansion of Atlantes : but the ring, which discovered what was before invisible, could not, though it revealed this paradise, enable Agramant or his followers to enter it. So steep and smooth was the rock by nature, that none could scale it; and even Brunello was obliged to renounce the attempt. He did not, however, for this, despair of accomplishing the object of the enterprise; and, having obtained Agramant's approbation, caused the assembled courtiers and knights to celebrate a tournament upon the plain below. This was done with the view of seducing Rogero from his fastness, and the stratagem was attended with success.

Rogero joins the tourney, presented by Brunello with Sacripant's horse, Frontilatte, (whose name is afterwards changed into Frontino,) and with Balisarda, the sword of Orlando. In the medley he is treacherously wounded, but avenges himself of the traitor; and, returning to the summit of the mountain, is healed by the skill and attention of Atlantes, having previously learned from Brunello the preparations which were making for the invasion of France, and having indeed received his horse and arms, as an earnest for his service in the expedition.

The author now leaves him again on the mountain of Carena, to accompany Orlando and Brandimart.

These two, having separated from Rinaldo, Astolpho, and the rest, were pursuing their journey through India, when they found themselves near a stone, situated by a fountain, where sate a lady, having her eyes fixed upon the ground, while a bridge, which divided two roads hard by, was kept by an armed knight.

While Orlando and Brandimart were engaged in a friendly contest, who should first encounter him, a pilgrim advanced towards the bridge, notwithstanding the prohibition of him who kept it; and finding that the knight approached in order to enforce his threat, cast off his pilgrim's slough, and showed that he was armed cap-a-pe. A fierce combat now ensued, between him and the warder of the bridge, whom both Brandimart and Orlando thought they had seen before, but could not recognise, through the strangeness of his disguise. In this strife the pilgrim at last succeeded in making the warder give ground, and retire slowly from his post.

On the other side of the bridge, and near the fountain which formed the stream, was a monument, which an inscription proclaimed to be the sepulchre of Narcissus.

Contemplating himself in the neighbouring fountain, he had pined away; and his death was productive of new calamities. The fairy Silvanella, as her evil destiny would have it, passing near the body, fell in love with the dead youth, whom she entombed in this mausoleum of alabaster. Here, too, consumed by hopeless passion, she perished, and left this dying curse upon the waters; that who contemplated them should see pourtrayed there such a vision of beauty, that they should become incapable of departing from the place.

Many, who had arrived upon the banks of the river, in consequence of her malediction, remained gazing upon the stream, till they expired. Among these was the gentle king Larbiho, who came there with his leman Calidora, who remained inconsolable for his loss, and took up her dwelling in the meadow, where he died. This is she, who sits weeping by the water-side, and whose champion maintains the bridge against all comers.

And such was the tale she told Orlando, whom she conjured, in favour of her pious intentions, to aid her cavalier, hard pressed by the pilgrim.

Orlando, moved by her prayer, thrust himself between the combatants, whom he separated, and recognized one for Sacripant, and the other for Isoliero. Isoliero had accompanied the lady from Spain to India, for the purpose of rendering her this service; and Sacripant had been dispatched (as was said) by Angelica, to king Gradasso, for assistance, towards whose kingdom he was now upon his way.

When the count had learned from this monarch the object of his journey, and the peril of Angelica, he fled with Brandimart, from the dangerous water, mindful of the fate of those that had perished there; leaving Isoliero, who had been severely wounded by Sacripant, in the company of Calidora.

While Orlando took his way to Albracca, Sacripant took up the pilgrim's garb and staff, and pursued his towards the kingdom of Gradasso.

Orlando, arriving before Albracca, finds it closely beleaguered. He, however, makes his way into the citadel, and relates his adventures to Angelica, from the time of his departure, up to his separation from Rinaldo and the rest, when they departed to the assistance of Charlemagne. Angelica, in return, described the distresses of the garrison, and the force of the besiegers; and in conclusion, prayed Orlando to favour her escape from the pressing danger, and escort her into France. Orlando, who did not suspect that love for Rinaldo, who had returned thither, was her secret motive, joyfully agreed to the proposal, and the sally was resolved.

Leaving lights burning in the fortress, they departed at night-fall, and passed in safety through the enemy's camp. On the ensuing day, however, the besiegers discovered the deceit, stormed and sacked the citadel, and then pursued the deserters.

Of these, Orlando went first, escorting Angelica and Flordelis, while Brandimart covered their retreat. In consequence of this arrangement, Brandimart was separated one night from his companions, while Orlando and the two damsels were advancing on their way.

As these last, sorely tormented by hunger, were entering a valley at sunset, they saw, at the other extremity, a party of Lestrigonians, seated at their supper, and immediately galloped towards them; Orlando first, but followed by the damsels. Arriving amongst these cannibals, he prayed them, either for courtesy or hire, to give them food; and, being received with a feigned hospitality, had already dismounted from his horse, in order to take some refreshment, when the leader of the party, coming behind him, dealt a blow with his club, that laid him senseless on the ground. The damsels, who had just come up, terrified at this catastrophe, fled different ways, pursued by a party of the Lestrigonians.

During this time, the. others had stript Orlando of his arms; and were handling him, to see if he was fat, when he was awakened by the operation. Possessing himself of Durindana, he soon cleared the field of the cannibals, and was seeking an outlet from the valley, when he recognized Angelica, hunted by those who had pursued her and Flordelis. To save her, and avenge her of the miscreants, was the work of a moment.

It was said that the two damsels separated in their flight; in directing which, chance conducted each towards her natural protector; for Flordelis, flying east, whilst Angelica fled west, galloped towards a wood, where Brandimart was sleeping, after having long sought his companions in vain. Brandimart was as prompt in rescuing her, as Orlando was in saving Angelica. It is needless to describe his transports on this occasion : these were, however, of short duration; and he heard, with the bitterest regret, the narrative of Flordelis, who, relating what she believed she had witnessed, informed him she had left Orlando dead upon the field.

Returning with Brandimart towards the spot where she had left the count, a strange adventure for a long time delayed their search; for they had not ridden far, before they fell in with a cavalier on foot, unarmed, except as to his sword, who defied

Brandimart to battle; and while he, in a spirit of generosity, refused the challenge, snatched Flordelis from her palfrey, and running up a steep rock with his burden, threatened to throw her down a precipice, unless Brandimart ransomed her with his armour and his steed.

As Brandimart's armour rendered it impossible for him to pursue, he consented to the sacrifice; and the stranger appropriated the spoils. This was Marphisa, who had thrown by her arms, in order to pursue Brunello, and who, finding the chace hopeless, took this method to equip herself anew.

Brandimart, now reduced to his tunick, and deprived of his courser, mounted the damsel's palfrey, seated her on the croup, and proceeded on his way.

They were doomed to experience new dangers and interruptions. For journeying thus, they fell in with a band of robbers, from whom Brandimart fled, in the hope of finding some means of defence. His hope was realized; for, penetrating a wood, he arrived at a fountain, near which a king lay dead, who was armed cap-a-pe. Providing himself with his sword, Brandimart turned to bay, and soon made his pursuers repent of their temerity. These slain or put to flight, he clothed himself reluctantly in the other arms of the monarch, leaving him his crown and regal ornaments. This king was no other than Agrican, so preserved by a visible miracle.

An after-combat with the captain of these corsairs put the knight in possession of a steed, and thus re-equipt, he accompanied Flordelis in search of Orlando.

This paladin, having recovered Angelica (as has been related) had journeyed as far homeward as the sea-coast of Syria without impediment. Here he found a vessel ready to carry the king of Damascus, Norandino, to the island of Cyprus, where he was to make his first essay of arms.

This was to be made for love of a lady whose name was Lucina, and whose father, Tibiano was king of Cyprus. This sovereign had proclaimed a tournament, of which the princess was to be the prize, and thither went Norandino, who invited

Orlando to accompany him. The count, disguising his name and country, and feigning himself a Circassian, called Rotolante, accepted the offer, and, together with Angelica, joined Norandino, who was accompanied by a brilliant train of adventurers. He was scarcely on ship-board before a breeze sprang up from the land, and the galley was under sail.

For the tournament which was preparing, many Greeks and many Pagans had assembled, among whom were Basaldo and Morbeco, Turks, and Gostanzo a Greek. This Gostanzo was the son of Vataron, emperor of Constantinople, and had brought Gryphon and Aquilant in his company, who, together with Origilla, had sought the hospitality of the Grecian court.

In the tourney the combatants are ranged under the banner of this Gostanzo on the one side, and that of Norandino on the other. Gryphon and Aquilant serve under the first, and Orlando under the second. They are, however, disguised from each other by borrowed devices, and Gryphon only suspects a knight who bore away the honors of the first day, to be Orlando, from his superior prowess, and from the presence of Angelica, whom he had observed seated amongst the ladies that honoured the spectacle with their presence.

Imparting his suspicions to Gostanzo after the trumpets had blown to lodging, the wily Greek determined to rid himself of so formidable an adversary. He accordingly introduced himself secretly to Orlando, and informed him of a treason which (as he said) the king of Cyprus meditated against him, at the instigation of Ganelon, offering him at the same tune the means of escape. This was a pinnace moored in a creek, in which Orlando, breathing vengeance against the Maganzese, embarked with Angelica, for France.

Disembarking in Provence, they pursued their way by land, and arriving hot, and weary, in the forest of Arden, where Rinaldo had lately drunk of the fountain of Love, chance directed Angelica to the waters of Disdain, of which she drank.

Issuing thence, the count and damsel encountered a stranger knight. This was no other than Rinaldo, who had missed

Rodomont, then engaged in combat with Ferrau; and who, on a nearer approach, recognised Angelica with joy, though his new arms and ensigns disguised Orlando, who accompanied her. The consequences of such a meeting are easily foreseen. Angelica views Rinaldo with disgust, and a new cause of strife is kindled between the kinsmen.

Terrified at the combat which ensued, Angelica fled amain through the forest, and came out upon a plain, covered with tents. This was the camp of Charlemagne, who led the army of reserve, destined to support the troops which had advanced to oppose the descent of Rodomont. Charles, having heard the damsel's tale, with difficulty separates the two cousins, and then consigns Angelica, as the cause of quarrel, to the care of Namus duke of Bavaria, promising she shall be his who best deserves her, in the first battle with the Saracens.

The author here returns to Agramant, who was left holding a tournament at the foot of Mount Carena in Africa. He having heard of the knight who was slain, and that, contrary to his orders, (which were only to employ courteous weapons,) determined to take vengeance upon his murderer, and supposing Brunello to be the criminal, (since Rogero had appeared with his arms and steed,) ordered him to be hanged upon the spot.

The danger of him who was about to suffer for his sake, now again brought "Rogero from his retreat. He routed the troops appointed to watch over the execution, rescued Brunello, and then, presenting himself to Agramant, related every thing as it had passed.

Agramant, too happy to find the object of his search in the youth who had performed such wonders, forgave the death of the slaughtered cavalier, knighted Rogero, and carried him off to Biserta, where his vassal kings and barons assembled for the invasion of Christendom.

While they are in the midst of their revelry, a messenger reports the return of Rodomont's fleet, whose followers brought with them, as a prisoner, Dudon the Dane; but could give no account of Rodomont their leader.

He was this while engaged in battle with Ferrau, with whom we left him quarrelling about Doralice; but their strife was soon interrupted by the arrival of a messenger, who brought news that Marsilius was, at the instigation of Ganelon, besieging Mount Albano. On hearing this, the duellists make peace, and ride together to join the besiegers.

On their way they fall in with Vivian and Malagigi, sons of duke Aymon, of Mount Albano, who are proceeding towards Paris, to demand succour of Charlemagne; and Malagigi, retiring with Vivian into a wood, performs a magic rite, by which he ascertains the design of the approaching warriors Rodomont and Ferrau. To frustrate this, he conjures up a bevy of fiends, armed and mounted as knights, divides them into two squadrons, takes the command of one himself, and gives that of the other to Vivian. Thus accompanied, the Christian knights charge their adversaries. But the Pagans are too strong for them, take Malagigi and Vivian prisoners, and send their demons howling back to hell.

Here the author exclaims,
But that I would not seem with folly tainted,
I own I would have fain beheld the attack;
So great is my desire to be acquainted
With those the wizard brought his cause to back :
And prove with my own eyes, if truly painted,
The devil be so very foul and black;
More; that his pictures differ as to nail,
And horn, and hoof, and length and breadth of tail.

To return to the story, Rodomont and Ferrau arrive in the Spanish camp before Mount Albano, which is shortly afterwards attacked by the army of Charlemagne. Divers feats of prowess are achieved on both sides; but the most interesting circumstance is a single combat between Rodomont and Bradamant; which the author breaks off in order to resume the story of Brandimart.

This knight, having obtained a steed and armour, as has been before related, proceeds with Flordelis towards Europe.

Thus journeying, the pair arrived in front of a magnificent palace. Here a damsel, standing in a balcony, motioned to them to take another way; but in vain; for Brandimart, feigning not to understand the purport of her signs, rode boldly up to the gate. He is now opposed by a giant, armed with a serpent, which he uses as a sword. Him the knight vanquishes after a long battle, in which he is opposed by a variety of enchantments; the giant and serpent exchanging forms, as one or the other is slain He next kills a knight who kept a sepulchre in the inner court, and opposed his further progress.

He and Flordelis, who had followed her lover, now seek the gate by which they had entered, but all appearance of it was lost.

While they are vainly seeking the means of escape, they are addressed by the damsel who had at first waved them from the palace; and who informed Brandimart, he must open the sepulchre, and kiss whatever issued from it, if he expected deliverance from his prison. Brandimart, little terrified by the injunction, promised compliance; but started back, and put his hand to his sword, on the appearance of a dragon. Reproached by the damsel of the castle for his breach of promise, he manned his spirits for the encounter, and kissed the monster in the mouth. A sudden cold ran through his bones at coming hi contact with her : but what was his surprise, on seeing the dragon trans formed into a beautiful damsel !

This was a fay so transmuted, who, grateful for her deliverance, offered to enchant the horse and arms of Brandimart, at the same time entreating him to conduct the lady of the castle, who was named Doristella, into Syria.

This promised, the gate re-appeared, the fay enchanted the steed and arms of Brandimart, and he, accompanied by the two ladies, departed upon the quest enjoined.

They had ridden some time in silence, when Doristella, rallying the knight for his taciturnity, proposed to beguile the way with the relation of her adventures. The offer was gratefully received, and the damsel began her story as follows :

"My father, king Doliston," said she, " had two daughters, the eldest of whom, while yet a child, was carried off by a thief from the shore of Lissa. Of this daughter, who was the promised spouse of Theodore the son of a neighbouring king, nothing was ever afterwards heard."

"And what was the name of the mother ?" exclaimed Flordelis; but Brandimart having checked her for her interruption, Doristella continued her narrative in her own way. " My intended brother-in-law," said the damsel, " still kept up his connection with my family, and he and I soon became mutually enamoured of one another. The young man at length unbosomed himself to my father, and demanded me in marriage; but my father, to his mortification, told him, that he had that very day promised me to the wretch, whom you slew in the palace.

"To this wretch, named Usbeck of Bursa, a Turcoman by nation, was I wedded; a man valiant in the field, but, as to the rest, little capable of winning a lady's love. This man, who was jealous in proportion to the grounds he gave me for disgust, was compelled to join an expedition against Vatarone the emperor of Greece. Departing, he left me in care of a slave called Gambone, a monster of deformity, whom he commanded never to stir from my side. He had not been long absent, when Theodore arrived at Bursa, and having corrupted Gambone, obtained access to my bed. Our intercourse was long continued, to our mutual satisfaction, when Usbeck arrived suddenly one night at Bursa, and demanded instant entrance into his house. Our courage did not desert us under these circumstances, and Theodore, slipping down stairs in the dark, escaped at the same time that Usbeck was admitted. Our danger, however, did not end here; for my husband's suspicions had been awakened by his detention at the door, and searching every part of my chamber, he found a mantle which my lover had left behind him in his retreat.

His suspicions being now confirmed, he burst into a transport of jealous fury, and ordered the slave Gambone for instant execution. According to the custom of the country, his other slaves were conducting him for that purpose, through the

134

city with a horn sounding before him, when Theodore met the procession, and falling upon the criminal, reproached him, amid a shower of blows, with having robbed him of his mantle.

This trick of Theodore's, who was unknown to Usbeck, saved the slave, and effaced the suspicions which he entertained of my fidelity. New offences, however, on my part, for I still continued my intercourse with Theodore, renewed his jealousy, and he at last shut me up in the enchanted palace whence you delivered me; though it was not then kept by the giant and serpent, which were the afterwork of a necromancer who wrought for him."

The damsel was here interrupted by an outcry, and the party was instantly set upon by thieves. These were, however, beaten off, and their leader taken — prisoner by Brandimart. He, throwing himself at the feet of the cavalier, entreated him not to carry him to Lissa, as he dreaded the vengeance of Doliston, the prince of that country, for having formerly carried off his eldest daughter, whom he had sold to the lord of the Sylvan Tower.

Brandimart, however, who has secret reasons (as will be shortly seen) for being pleased at this account, insists upon carrying him to Lissa; and arriving before Doliston's capital, finds it besieged by Theodore, in revenge for the monarch's having refused him Doristella. All now is cleared up. Flordelis turns out to be the missing daughter of Doliston, who had been wooed by Brandimart in the Sylvan Tower; and no further obstacle existing to the union of Theodore and Doristella, these two, as well as Brandimart and Flordelis, are united in marriage; Doliston and Theodore having previously made peace.

After long festivities in honour of these double espousals, Brandimart and Flordelis, still anxious to pursue Orlando, embark for France with a prosperous wind. This, however, changes; increases to a tempest; and finally drives them on the shores of Carthage. Here Brandimart, less anxious for his own safety than for that of Flordelis and his companions, conceals his being a Christian, and announcing himself only as son of Monodontes, king of the Distant Isles, declares that it was his purpose to visit Agramant in Biserta.

He accordingly sets off, always attended by Flordelis, for that capital; where he is magnificently received, and is afterwards carried off by Agramant, together with Rogero, on his expedition against France.

Agramant, leaving Dudon a prisoner at large in Biserta, which was to be governed in his absence by a vice-roy, embarks upon his long meditated enterprise, disembarks in Spain, and arrives, by forced marches, near Mount Albano, in the neighbourhood of which the armies of Charlemagne and Marsilius were left engaged.

The strife was still continued with unabated fury; and in this Rinaldo was matched with Ferrau, king Grandonio with the marquis Oliviero, Serpentine with Ogier the Dane, and Marsilius himself against Charlemagne.

These duels were, however, of little account, compared with that which raged between Rodomont and Bradamant. Of this desperate contest Orlando was a witness; who would not turn his arms against Rodomont while he was engaged with so formidable an adversary.

While Orlando thus played the part of a looker-on, he was surprised by the sound of an approaching enemy, and casting his eyes in that direction, saw a plump of spears, with banners and pennons, descending the sides of a mountain. He immediately stooped from his saddle to pick up a weighty lance which was lying on the ground, and thus prepared himself for the encounter of what proved to be the army of Agramant.

This sovereign had in the meantime dispatched one of his vassal kings, named Pinadoro, towards the field of battle, with orders to bring him one or more prisoners, who might inform him of the state of the Christian army. Pinadoro and Orlando meet and tilt together: but the feudatory king, instead of accomplishing the orders of his sovereign, remains the prisoner of the count He is, however, no sooner taken than liberated by his conqueror, who bids him return to his army in peace. The report of his ill success does not frighten Agraniant from his purpose; and the Moorish army descends like a torrent into the plain.

At the sight of these new enemies, Charles left Marsilius, who was closely pressed by him, and ordered Rinaldo also to give a respite to Ferrau, and lead a squadron against the approaching troops, whom he divined to be what they really were. Other divisions of the army followed in support of one another, and a bloody battle ensued, with various and very doubtful success. Meantime Orlando, who wished such measure of misfortune to Charlemagne as should make his assistance necessary, and ensure him the possession of Angelica as his reward, had retired from the medley into a neighbouring wood, and was praying devoutly for the discomfiture of the Christians. By accident, Ferrau, fatigued by his long contest with Rinaldo, and lately as hard pressed by him as Marsilius was by Charlemagne, had sought shelter in the same retreat Here, stooping to drink from the banks of a river, he dropt his helmet in the water, and was engaged in a vain attempt to recover it, when he was discovered by Orlando. The count, however, was too generous to attack an enemy under such disadvantages, and weakened as Ferrau evidently was by the combat he had previously waged against Rinaldo. He accordingly, after a short conference with him, in which he learned the state of things, spurred his courser, in order to join the army of Charlemagne.

Here he performs high feats of valour, and, after the slaughter of many adversaries, is advancing against Rogero, when Atlantes, who had accompanied the youth, (since he could not restrain him from following his destiny,) diverts Orlando from his object by the vision of a triumphant Pagan squadron, and of the personal danger of Charlemagne. Fascinated by this illusion, he follows the supposed Saracens into the forest of Arden. Here the vision disappears; and the count, wearied with the fruitless chace, lights from Brigliadoro near a fountain. Stooping to drink, he sees a crystal palace at the bottom, through the walls of which he beholds a dance of ladies, and, unable to resist the temptation of an adventure, plunges, armed as he is, into the fountain.

Book III.

Argument.

The third book opens with the introduction of a new character, Mandricardo, son of Agncan, the Tartar king, who, pursuing his way to France in order to avenge his father's death, is made the prisoner of a fairy. He frees himself, acquires the arms of Hector, and is, as well as other knights, involved in various adventures, till the story returns to the invasion of France, which is suddenly interrupted in the middle.

THE author opens this book by stating, that he is called away to the north. Here a mighty storm was gathering; and France, already sorebested, was suddenly threatened by a new storm from the remote quarter of Tartary.

The emperor of this region, named Mandricardo, having wasted it by his violences, was proceeding in a course of imperious tyranny, when an old man threw himself in his way, and, reproaching him with his outrages, bade him desist from warring upon the innocent and defenceless, and seek to revenge the death of his father upon one who was worthy of his wrath ; to wit, upon Orlando, the murderer of king Agrican.

Stung to the heart by the old man's repreaches, Mandricardo, determining to owe his success in the enterprise on which he resolved to his own individual valour, leaves his kingdom incognito, and departs, without horse or arms, towards the west. Travelling thus alone and a-foot, he had passed the confines of Armenia, when he spied upon a day a pavilion, pitched near a fountain; and imagining that he might there find what he was determined to win by force, entered it, with the view of searching for the horse and arms of which he stood in need. There was none to defend the entrance, and he was already within the pavilion, when a voice was heard to murmur from the waters, that he was a prisoner to the power, whose possession he had violated.

Mandricardo, however, heard not, or else disregarded the voice; and pursuing his search, found a suit of armour, disposed upon a carpet, and a courser fastened to a neighbouring pine.

He immediately clothed himself in the arms, and seized upon the steed, with which he was departing, when a fire suddenly sprang up before him, that, spreading itself, destroyed the pine, and left the fountain and pavilion alone untouched. Mandricardo is himself embraced by the flames, which destroy his armour and clothing even to his shirt. To escape the torture, he leaps from his horse, every thing which he had on him being consumed, and casts himself into the water. Here, he is received into the arms of a naked damsel of incomparable beauty, who kisses him, and bids him be of good cheer, informing him that he is taken in the snare of a fairy, but that if he has heart and discretion, he may rescue not only himself, but so many damsels and cavaliers, that he shall reap immortal glory from the achievement.

She pursued her story, informing him, that the fountain was the work of a fairy, who had imprisoned there king Gradasso of Sericane, Gryphon and Aquilant, and many other knights and ladies. "Beyond the hill," said she, "which you see before you, is situated a castle, where this fairy has laid up the arms of Hector, with the exception of his sword. On his being slain treacherously by Achilles, a queen, named Penthesilea, possessed herself of this. At her death it passed to Almontes, and from him was taken by Orlando. This weapon was called Durindana. The remainder of his arms was saved and carried off by AEneas, from whom they were received by her, in recompence of a marvellous service which she had bestowed upon him. If you have the courage to attempt the acquisition of these arms, secured in yonder castle by enchantment, I will be your guide."

Mandricardo was enraptured at the proposal, and only hesitated at the idea of exposing himself naked. This difficulty was, however, got over by the lady, who, letting down her hair, which was bound about her head in braids, furnished a complete covering for herself and the cavalier. Being sheltered from sight by this, they issued, linked arm in arm, from the water, and took their way together to the pavilion.

Entering this, which, as was said, remained untouched by the fire, they reposed for some time upon flowers. At length the damsel gave the signal for departure, and having clothed Mandricardo in armour, conducted him where a courser was in waiting. Upon this he leapt, all armed as he was; and the lady having mounted on a palfrey, both set forward on their enterprise.

They had ridden about a mile, when the damsel, explaining the dangers of the quest, informed Mandricardo that he would have to combat with Gradasso, the conqueror of Gryphon, who had at first maintained the field against all comers.

Thus speaking, they arrived at the castle, which was of alabaster, overlaid with gold. Before this, on a lawn, enclosed with a barrier of live myrtles, sat an armed knight on horseback, and who was no other than Gradasso. Mandricardo, upon seeing him, dropt his vizor, and laid his lance in the rest. The champion of the castle was as ready, and each spurred towards his opponent. They splintered their spears with equal force, and again returning to the charge, encountered with their swords. This contest was long and doubtful, when Mandricardo, determining to bring it to an issue, threw his arms about Gradasso, and the two horsemen, grappling together, tumbled to the ground. In the struggle, however, Mandricardo fell uppermost, and preserving his advantage, made Gradasso prisoner. The damsel now interfered, proclaiming the victory of the new comer, and consoling the vanquished as she could, for his discomfiture.

In the meantime, the sun had set upon the strife, and it was too late for Mandricardo to enter the enchanted castle, which the damsel informed him would be only accessible after sunrise. She invites him, therefore, to lie down amongst the flowers with which the meadow is enamelled, proffering to be his guard; but informs him, that there is harbourage to be obtained at a neighbouring castle, though it can only be purchased by exposure to notable peril. This, she says, is kept by a kind and courteous lady, who is often disturbed, in the exercise of her hospitality, by a giant named Malapresa, whom he would do well to avoid, as he has already sufficient toil and danger on his hands.

Mandricardo rejects this kind intimation, and insists upon being guided to the lady's lodging.

He and the damsel accordingly set off in that direction, and soon arrive at the palace, which is illuminated with a thousand lights. It appeared as if a watch was kept for friends or foes; and a dwarf was posted in a gallery over the entrance, whose duty it was to give notice of all comers. On the winding of his horn, if there were cause for suspicion, the household, armed with missile weapons, assembled in the balconies : but if it were an errant knight, in search of hospitality, damsels came forth to salute him, and conduct him into the castle.

In this manner was Mandricardo received, who was afterwards magnificently entertained by the lady of the mansion. Their festivity is, however, interrupted by the dwarf's horn, which sounds an alarum. The signal is hardly given, before Malapresa has forced the gate, and appears in the middle of the guests, armed with an enormous mace. A furious combat now ensues between him and the Tartar king, in which the giant is slain, and cast into the castle ditch. This event occasions only a short interruption of the festivity, which is prolonged late into the night. The revellers at length retire; and Mandricardo amongst the rest, who is as magnificently lodged, as he had been feasted, by the lady of the castle.

At sun-rise he starts from his couch, descends into the castle-garden, washes himself at a fountain; then puts on his armour, and, guided by his former conductress, proceeds upon his enterprise.

On arriving at the eastern entrance of the outer wall of the enchanted castle, which was not more magnificent than extensive, and which entrance Mandricardo found undefended, he was informed, that he must plight an oath upon the threshold, to touch a shield which was suspended. there from a pilaster of gold. The bearing of this was a white eagle on an azure field, in memory of the bird of Jove, who bore away Ganymede, the flower of the Phrygian race. Beneath was engraved the following legend :

Let none, with hand profane, my buckler wrong,

Unless he be himself as Hector strong.

The damsel immediately, alighting from her palfrey, inclined herself to the ground; the Tartar king bent himself with equal reverence, and afterwards passed the threshold without an obstacle.

Advancing through the eastern entrance of the enclosure towards the shield, Mandricardo touched it with his sword. An earthquake immediately shook the place, and the way by which he had entered closed. Another, and an opposite gate, however, opened, and displayed a field, bristling with stalks and grain of gold. The damsel upon this told him, that he who had entered had no means of departure but by cutting down the harvest which was before him, and in uprooting a tree which grew in the middle of the field. The champion, without answering, prepared himself, for his work, and immediately began to mow the harvest with his sword. A strange effect followed; and every grain was instantly transformed into some ravenous animal, lion, panther, or unicorn, who all flew in fury at the reaper.

Mandricardo, thus assailed, snatched up a stone, without knowing what virtue resided in it, and cast it amongst the herd. This stone was party-coloured, green, vermilion, — white, azure and gold. A strange wonder followed : for it no sooner lighted amongst the beasts, than they turned their rage one against the other, and perished by mutual wounds. Mandricardo did not stop to marvel at the miracle, but proceeded to fulfil his task, and uproot the tree. This, which was lofty and full of leaves, he embraced by the trunk, making vigorous efforts to tear it up by the roots. At each of these fell a shower of leaves, which were instantly changed into birds of prey, who attacked the knight, as the beasts had done before. Undismayed, however, by this new annoyance, he continued to tug at the trunk till it yielded to his efforts. A burst of wind and thunder followed, and the hawks and vultures were dispersed.

These, however, only gave place to a new foe; for from the hole made by tearing up the tree, issued a furious serpent with many tails, who darted at Mandricardo, wound herself about his limbs, and was about to devour him. Fortune, however, again stood his friend; for, writhing under the folds of the monster, and struggling to free himself, he fell backwards into the hole, and his enemy was crushed beneath his weight.

Mandricardo, when he had somewhat recovered from the shock, and assured himself of the destruction of the dragon, began to contemplate the place into which he had fallen, and saw that he was in a vault, encrusted with costly metals, and illuminated by a live coal. In the middle was a sort of ivory bier, and upon this was extended, what appeared to be a knight in armour, but what was in truth, an empty trophy, composed of the rich and precious arms, once Hector's, and to which nothing was wanting but the sword. While Mandricardo stood contemplating the prize, a door opened behind him, and a bevy of fair damsels entered dancing, who bore him away to the place where the shield was suspended, and where he found the fairy of the castle seated in state. By her he was invested with the arms which he had won, he first swearing, at her injunction, to wear no other blade but the sword Durindana, which he was to ravish from Orlando, and thus complete the conquest of Hector's arms.

The adventure was now accomplished, and the champion departed in order to achieve die great purpose, for which he left his realm of Tartary. Many illustrious knights issued at the same tune from the dungeons of the fairy, who had remained prisoners on a failure of their enterprise, and who had been now liberated by his success. Amongst these were Gradasso, Isolier, Sacripant, Gryphon, and Aquilant, with many others.

Mandricardo himself pursued his journey, in company with GradasSo. Of the others, Gryphon and Aquilant, who knew the language of the Saracens, travelled through strange countries; and thus journeying along the sea-shore, fell in with two damsels, the one clothed in white, and the other in black, and attended by two dwarfs. As the colour of their respective ladies, such was that of their dwarfs, and of the palfreys which they rode : saving in this, they were so alike, as to be undistinguishable one from the other; and were equals in beauty and grace.

"Sister," said one of these, addressing herself to her companion, " there is no defence against destiny; yet wisdom may in some sort, controul fortune : then let us detain these, at least awhile, from the fate which is reserved for them in France." Thus spoke the sable to the white dasmel, unheard of the two knights who were approaching, and who saluted them with all the courtesy due to their bearing and appearance.

One of the ladies demanded a boon of the two cavaliers; who both as instantly vowed to perform whatever was enjoined them. This was to take the field against a miscreant, named Orrilo, engendered of a goblin and fairy, who inhabited a tower upon the Nile, where he kept (says the story) a kind of dragon, termed a crocodile, and fed it with human flesh. The damsels go on to state, that hitherto no one has been able to prevail against the wretch, who, in dying, renews himself like the phoenix. This account does not discourage the brothers, who again proffer their assistance.

Aquilant accordingly encounters Orrilo, where he keeps the way against travellers; and he being sore pressed, flies to the tower, and turns out his crocodile.

Gryphon now deems himself justified in assisting his brother; and the crocodile is at length slain. Orrilo, however, though often worsted, appears to be irresistible : for though he is frequently unhorsed, and is actually severed into two parts by one of the brothers, he constantly re-unites himself, and renews the contest. The day is now closing, and the two .brothers are in despair.

While things are in this state, a new performer appears upon the theatre. This is a knight, who dragged a giant captive: but here the author leaves Gryphon and Aquilant, as well as the knight and his prisoner, and resumes the story of Mandricardo and Gradasso, who were left journeying together towards France.

This pair, after traversing various regions, arrive upon the sea-coast, where they find a lady chained and exposed upon the beach. On their interrogating her, she tells them, that she awaits the approach of a furious Ork, who will devour her alive; and entreats them, as an act of compassion, rather to put her to an immediate death, than to leave her exposed to so horrible a fate. The only favour that she requests of them, besides this dreadful grace, is, (should they fall in with him,) to inform Norandino, king of Damascus, of her death, and dying sentiments of affection to him.

The knights, however, insist on defending her, and a dreadful conflict ensues between them and the Ork, who is represented as something indistinct, monstrous and gigantic. Gradasso is soon overpowered, and Mandricardo, who, in conformity to his vow, was unprovided with a sword, is obliged to fly before the pest.

He, however, finds his deliverance in flight; for, speeding his steps along the cliffs, he arrives at a frightful chasm, at which he springs in utter desperation. The Ork following him, is unable to clear it, and tumbles down the abyss.

Mandricardo quit of his foe, descends to the shore, in search of Gradasso and Lucina, (for so was named the lady chained to the rock,) and proceeds in company with them along the beach. From this they behold a ship in the distance, which bears the flag of Tibiano, king of Cyprus and Rhodes, the father of Lucina, and who was then seeking his daughter. Lucina, overjoyed at the sight, makes a signal of her vest, and waves the galley to the land. On board this she embarks, together with her defenders; but the vessel has scarcely shown her stern to the shore, when the Ork re-appears, with a monstrous fragment of a mountain on his shoulders : This he heaves into the sea, which flashes above her topmast head, and all cower at the bottom of the vessel for refuge; but the mass misses the mark at which it was hurled, and a loud land-wind rising at the moment, the vessel is blown off to sea.

One danger is only substituted for another; the storm increases, and all is darkness and dismay. In this situation, the night closes in, during which they drift at the mercy of the winds. The succeeding day dawns upon them under better auspices; and they find themselves, in the morning, upon the shore of Acquamorta, where a mountain separates France and Spain.

Here they land in the neighbourhood of a cave, called Runa, without having any knowledge of the coast upon which they are cast. Leaving there Tibiano and Lucina, Graclasso and Mandricardo proceed, armed and mounted, in search of intelligence.

They have not proceeded far, before they hear the noise of battle, and pushing their horses towards the sound, find Agramant engaged with Charlemagne.

The main story is thus brought back to the point where the Christian and paynim armies were left, and where the tide of conquest was fluctuating between the hostile forces. Retiring from the medley, Ferrau had withdrawn into a neighbouring wood, and was fishing for his helmet, in a stream in which he had lost it as he stooped to drink. At this period fortune declares decisively in favour of the infidels; and, while Rogero and Rinaldo are engaged in a single combat on foot, Charlemagne's forces give way at all points, in irreparable confusion.

The duel of the two champions is interrupted by the crowd of fugitives and pursuers; and Rinaldo, now seeing Bayardo loose in the field, attempts to get possession of him. The horse, however, will not be taken; and Rinaldo, following him into a thick wood, is left there by the author, who returns to Rogero.

Rogero was also a-foot, and grieving for the loss of his own horse, Frontino, whom he however recovered in the rout. He now finds Bradamant and Rodomont engaged in combat. Though he knew not who they were, he could distinguish that one was a paynim, and the other a Christian; and, moved by the spirit of courtesy, approached them, and exclaimed, "Let him of the two, who worships Christ, pause, and hear what I have to say. The army of Charles is routed, and in flight; so that if he wishes to follow his leader, he has no time for delay." Bradamant, who is thunderstruck with the tidings, desires immediately to leave the field; but this is refused by her antagonist : and Rogero, indignant at his discourtesy, insists upon her departure, while he takes up the quarrel with Rodomont.

This, long and obstinately maintained on both sides, is interrupted by the return of Bradamant, who, not being able to overtake the fugitives, and being divided in her feelings, as to what she owed on the one side to her emperor, and on the other to the stranger who had so generously taken her part, yields at last to what was the stronger impulse, and comes back to his assistance.

She arrives, however, when he was least in need of it; and when he had smote his enemy such a blow, as obliged him to drop both his sword and bridle. Rogero, however, disdaining to profit by his defenceless situation, sate apart upon his horse, whilst that of Rodomont bore his rider, stunned and stupefied, about the field. Rogero was at this juncture approached by Bradamant; who conceived a yet higher notion of his valour, on beholding such an instance of forbearance. She addressed him, by excusing herself for leaving him exposed to an enemy from his interference in her cause, pleading her attachment to her sovereign as the motive; and was engaged in conference with him, when Rodomont recovered from his confusion. His bearing was however changed, and he disclaimed all thoughts of further contest with one of who he said, had already vanquished him by his courtesy." So saying, he quitted his antagonist, picked up his sword, and spurred out of sight.

Bradamant was now again desirous of retiring from the field, and Rogero insisted on accompanying her, though yet unconscious of her sex.

As they pursued their way, she enquired the name and quality of her new associate; and Rogero informed her of his nation and family. Beginning from the destruction of Troy, he told her that Astyanax, who was preserved by a stratagem of the Greeks, having established the kingdom of Messina, in Sicily, perished by the treachery of a priest, named AEgystus. The widow of this prince, being then big with child, flying from her enemies, escaped to Rheggio. Here she brought forth a son, who was christened Polydore. From this Polydore descended Polydantes, and from, him twin branches, who gave origin to two other families of renown. From one of these sprang the royal race of Pepin and Charlemagne; and from the other, two illustrious, houses, one of which took root at Rheggio, (' once called Risa') and the other at Ancona. "From that of Rheggio am I derived," continu-. ed he; "and am son of Rogero, the son of Agolant and Gallicella. She flying when big with me, from a horrible persecution which she endured during the absence of her husband, then, engaged in war, brought me forth in a foreign land, and died in giving me life. It was here that a magician took charge of me, who trained me to feats of arms amidst the dangers of the desert and of the chace."

Having thus ended his tale, Rogero entreated a similar return of courtesy from his companion; who replied, without disguise, that she was of the race of Clermont, and sister to Rinaldo, the fame of whom was perhaps known to him. Rogero, much moved by this intelligence, entreats her to take off her helmet; and, at the discovery of her face, remains transported with pleasure.

Whilst he is contemplating this with rapture, an unexpected danger hangs over the future lovers. A party which was placed in a wood, in order to intercept the retreating Christians, breaks from its ambush upon the pair; and Bradamant, who was uncasqued, is wounded in the head. Rogero is in fury at this attack; and Bradamant, replacing her helmet, joins him in taking speedy vengeance on their enemies. Of these they clear the field, but separate in the pursuit; and the author first resumes the story of Rogero.

Quitting the chace, and wandering by hill and vale, in search of her whom he had no sooner found than lost, Rogero now falls in with two knights, whom he joins, and who promise to assist him in the search of his companion, whose arms he describes, concealing, from a vague feeling of jealousy, her quality and sex.

It was evening when they joined company, and having journeyed together through the night, the morning was beginning to break, when one of the strangers, fixing his eyes upon Rogero's shield, demanded of him by what right he bore the device pourtrayed upon it. Rogero, in return interrogated the enquirer as to his pretensions to the bearing of Hector, who proclaimed himself to be Mandricardo, declared how he had won it, and proposed that arms should decide which of the two was most worthy to bear the symbol of the Trojan knight.

Rogero felt no other objection to this proposal, than die scruple which rose out of the observation, that his antagonist was without a sword. Mandricardo, however, insisted that this need be no impediment; and then informed him of the vow which he had taken, never to wear a sword till he had completed the acquisition of Hector's arms by the conquest of Durindana.

This was no sooner said, than a new antagonist started up in Gradasso, in whom the reader will have recognised the companion of Mandricardo. Gradasso now vindicates his prior right to the quest of Durindana, to obtain which he had embarked (as was related in the beginning) in that fearful war upon France. A quarrel is thus kindled between the kings of Tartary and Sericane. Mondricardo uproots a young elm-tree, to supply the place of a, sword; and Gradasso, disdaining to combat with unequal weapons, arms himself with a pine. Being thus furnished for offence, they encounter . one another with fury, while Rogero laughs and looks upon the strife.

He, nevertheless, several times attempts to separate the combatants, but always without success. While the conflict is thus raging, a knight arrives upon the ground, accompanied by a damsel, to whom Rogero relates the cause and progress of the strife. This turns out to be Brandimart," accompanied by Flordelis. He also interposes his mediation, and succeeds better in bringing the two champions to accord. This he effects, by informing them that he can conduct them to the presence of Orlando, the master of Durindana.

"If," said he, " you can heal him of a strange enchantment, it is from him that you may claim the sword; nor is he one who will refuse you a fair field for obtaining it. Two leagues from hence," continued Brandimart, " is a water, called the River of Laughter, but which would be better entitled the Stream of Tears. Here Orlando is enchanted. An African magician made this known to me, and I had already disposed myself to free him, or perish by his side, but being insufficient by myself for such an enterprise, Heaven has willed that I should light upon you to assist me in the attempt."

Gradasso and Mandricardo instantly make truce, in order to accompany Brandimart in his quest, nor will Rogero be left behind.

This resolution, however, gave rise to a serious difficulty; for the number to be employed in the adventure was to be unequal, as Brandimart was instructed; and one must therefore necessarily be rejected. Who should lie rejected, it was now determined to decide by lot; and chance pronounced against Mandricardo, who departed with reluctance from the field, and wandering long, arrived at last in Agramant's camp, who had sate down before Paris.

The story of Orlando is now resumed, where it was left by the author at the conclusion of the second book. The count having plunged into the fountain, termed the River of Laughter, is so delighted with the company of Naiads, and with the pleasures which he finds beneath the waters, that he remains there a willing prisoner.

About this water extended an enchanted wood, thick with evergreen trees; and here arrived Rogero, Gradasso, Brandimart, and Flordelis, determined to attempt the deliverance of Orlando.

This forest seemed impenetrable; but by the advice of Flordelis, the knights descended from their horses, and determined to cut themselves a passage. Rogero, in pursuance of this resolution, hews down a laurel with his sword. The tree is no sooner overthrown, than a beautiful damsel starts from its trunk, and claims the compassion of the knight. She informs him, that the trees which he beholds, as well as that which he has felled, contain sister nymphs, the victims of enchantment; the nature of which is such, that they remain transformed till liberated, as she had been, by the destruction of the plant in which they are imprisoned. " This deliverance is, however, as yet incomplete," pursued the damsel; " and, to perfect it, you must accompany me to the water, if you would not see me again rooted in the forest." Rogero yields to her prayer, accompanies her to the water, and, seduced by the enchantment, leaps hand in hand with her into the fountain.

In the meantime, Gradasso, attempting to clear his way, cuts down an ash, which is converted into a courser. He immediately mounts it; when the horse transports him through the air, and plunges with him into the enchanted stream, where he remains a prisoner with the rest.[25]

Brandimart, counselled by Flordelis, pursues the adventure with better success; and resisting every species of temptation which is presented to him, at length arrives at the banks of the fountain. Here, however, he would have yielded to the same fascination as the others, but for the wise precautions of Flordelis,

Who, for a safeguard, round his brow disposes
A mystic garland of enchanted roses,[26]

She had also furnished him with the same ornaments for the others whom he was to deliver from the pool. Armed with these wreaths, he approaches the knights, whom he finds in the bowers of crystal, into which he plunged, and crowns them with the garlands. The charm forthwith operates; their perverse inclination ceases, and they gladly return with their deliverer to the surface.

They are scarcely safe from the spell, when Gradasso bethinks him of his long quest, and a fierce battle ensues between him and Orlando, for the possession of Durindana. They are, however, induced to suspend this by the instances of their companions, and the entreaties of a stranger dwarf, who appears,

---

[25] The reader will see in this adventure, more especially in the author's fitting the temptations to the character of the knights, the hint which Tasso turned to so much better account in his creation of the forest of Armida.

[26] The idea of roses being a solvent of enchantments, is as old as Apuleius and Lucian ; and, like most of the mysticisms to be found in those authors, is probably to be traced to a much more ancient source.

mounted on a palfrey, and entreats the assistance of some of the knights.

These accordingly divide; Orlando, attended by Brandimart and Flordelis, taking his way towards Paris, and Rogero and Gradasso accompanying the dwarf.

The author accompanies Orlando and his friends, who arrive before Paris, besieged by the forces of Agramant, amid whose ranks were to be found assembled, Rodomont, Mandricardo, Ferrau, the newly arrived Gradasso, and all the worthies of the paynim army. Flordelis now retires into a wood for safety, while the two champions approach the camp of the besiegers. At this crisis Charlemagne makes a desperate sally, which is seconded by Orlando and Brandimart, and the fortune of the day seems balanced between the contending troops.

The author here leaves things thus suspended, and takes up the story of Bradamant, who lately separated form Rogero, in repulsing the ambuscade of the paynims. She journeying alone, and still suffering from her wound, at length reaches a hermitage, the tenant of which examines her head, cuts off her hair and with this bandages, and finally heals the gash which she had received.

Departing from his hermitage, and still pursuing her way alone, she alights from her horse, and reposes herself in a wood, where she is surprised sleeping by Flordespina, who, deceived by the appearance of her hair, takes her for a man. This princess, who was engaged with her damsels in the chase, by a stratagem detains Bradamant in the forest, where they pursue their sports in company.

But, exclaims the poet, while I sing these lays of ladies and of loves, I see France arming against Italy, and the horizon bright with flames. Hereafter, if it shall be permitted me I will piece the tale which I leave unfinished.

So ends the story of the Orlando Innamarato.

"To-morrow to fresh woods and pastures new."

www.ingramcontent.com/pod-product-compliance
Lightning Source LLC
Chambersburg PA
CBHW050409030726
47503CB00006B/2103